Recovery WITHOUT Relapse

EXPERIENCING LASTING TRIUMPH
OVER LIFE'S TRIGGERS

DR. GEORGE T. CRABB D.O. **&** BENJAMIN R. BURKS

Published by: Reformers Unanimous International Publishing
© 2013 by Reformers Unanimous Recovery Ministries NFP

Reformers Unanimous Recovery Ministries
PO Box 15732, Loves Park, IL 61132
Visit our website at www.reformersrecovery.com
Printed in Canada

Edited by: Wendy Burks
Cover & Interior Design by: David White

       Crabb, George 1965 -
       Benjamin R Burks 1964 -
       Recovery without Relapse

ISBN 978-1-61623-567-3

2nd EDITION

Table OF *Contents*

1. Recovery Without Relapse - Does It Exist? 4

2. Freedom, Not Sobriety, is the Goal 30

3. Relapse Is Not Part of Recovery 45

4. It Can Be You 51

5. An Ending Appeal 90

Appendix A: Matt's Testimony 95

Appendix B: Enter Not Into Temptation 103

Appendix C: Getting Down To the Heart of the Matter 121

Chapter 1

Recovery without Relapse - Does it Exist?

WE WRITE THIS BOOK IN HOPES of demonstrating to you how Reformers Unanimous can lead you into a recovery – from your alcoholism, drug addiction, or other destructive behaviors – that does not include relapse. We make this statement based on the results that we have achieved at Reformers Unanimous. At Reformers Unanimous, we assist people everyday in finding the Truth that makes them free, finally! We don't cure them; we show them the cure, which is the Truth. You, too, can be introduced to this cure today if you so desire.

Most of us have felt this same discouragement, suffered the same shame, experienced the same hardships, seen the same devastation on friendships and family and watched our loved ones and friends continue to spiral down in this viscous cycle called addiction. As we have watched, almost helplessly, our hearts are broken and our spirits are dashed. Our family members and loved ones have been in and out of treatment programs, and each treatment program has had certain suggestions. However, in nearly every case, their suggestions were directed at creating an environment where the individual would be less apt to use alcohol, drugs or participate in their destructive behavior. Nothing more definitive is ever given. You leave without the answer.

Truly, most individuals that are caught up in this vicious cycle of addictive behavior want to stop. They do desire normalcy again in their lives. But, they have a hard time putting their desires into reality. There is a freedom that exists for every person, and that freedom will make the individual whole in every way body, soul, and spirit. Yes, you, your loved one and your friend can be reclaimed from the abyss called addiction. Most individuals caught up in this vicious cycle of addition have been told the following lie so frequently that they believe it as the truth. The lie is this: ALCHOLISM AND DRUG ADDICTION AS WELL AS ALL OTHER DESTRUCTIVE BEHAVIORS ARE INCURABLE DISEASES. Because the same individuals that are listening to this lie have experienced relapses many times, they don't believe that true freedom is possible. My friend, do not be hesitant; do not be afraid to believe that you can experience freedom now and forever!

We at Reformers Unanimous want to help you lose that horrible, destructive image of yourself as incurably diseased alcoholics and drugs addicts and replace it with one that is pure, whole and forever free of addictive drugs and behavior. Whether it be at the Men's or Women's Discipleship Homes in Rockford, Illinois or in one of the over 700 local chapters around the world, we see the individuals confidence begin to grow as they come to understand a new way of life that is founded on the Truth; a new way of life that has eliminated the bondage of destructive behaviors; a new way of life that is full of the demonstration of joy, peace, longsuffering, gentleness, goodness, faith, meekness and temperance; a new life that truly acknowledges Romans 8:28 – *"And we know that all things work together for good to them that love God, to them who are the called according to his purpose;"* a new life where we see our past in the light of the glorious gospel of the Truth and that our past is exactly that, our past, and that our past is a part of our lives where we can now live and grow thereby. Our new identity is in the present; our new identity is in the Truth.

It is always a blessing for someone who is already walking in freedom see someone join them in that walk of freedom as they believe in the Truth and walk in the Truth with complete sobriety without fear of relapse. We want you to know that here at Reformers Unanimous we are in the trenches with you. It is of the utmost importance that you believe that what we are going to share with you in this book is the major factor in achieving your recovery free from relapse and that major factor is the Truth. As you believe, so it will be for you for our beliefs define our lives. Proverbs 23:7 says, *"For as he thinketh in his heart, so is he."* What you believe will be the key factors in your recovery without relapse. Permanent sobriety and everlasting joy will be yours!

Reformers Unanimous is based on a **Ten-Principle program,** written by Founder Steve Curington, as follows:

Step #1
IF GOD'S AGAINST IT, SO AM I!

"Now the works [deeds] *of the flesh* [humans] *are manifest* [revealed], *which are these; Adultery* [sex with someone other than your wife/husband], *fornication* [sex outside of marriage], *uncleanness* [sexual impurity], *lasciviousness* [sexual excess], *Idolatry* [things in your life that are more important than God], *witchcraft* [sorcery], *hatred, variance* [causing strife or discord], *emulations* [being jealous], *wrath* [sinful anger], *strife* [selfish ambition], *seditions* [dissentions], *heresies* [organized divisions or cliques], *Envyings, murders, drunkenness, revellings* [excessive eating], *and such like: of the which I tell you before, as I have also told you in time past, that they which do such things shall not inherit the kingdom of God." (Galatians 5:19-21)*

Throughout the Bible we see passages indicating behavior that God is against. He has asked that we avoid behaving in this way. He warns that participating in certain behavior will bring sorrow, punishment, and can even lead to a shorter life. We have seen this to be true in not only our own lives, but in the lives of many others as well. It is called the law of sowing and reaping. This simple law says if you sow (or spread) destructive behavior, you will reap (or receive) destruction in your life. But, if you spread good behavior patterns, you will receive blessings from God.

The Bible was written to tell us what is right, what is not right, how to get right, and how to stay right. If God's intention was to inform us of what is, what is not, how to get and stay right, then it is our responsibility to conform each area of our lives that is revealed to be wrong. God will help us to do this. He gives new believers His Spirit and a hunger to be right.

This new presence and new desire for good is what God uses to mold our new Christian character. If we draw a line and do not overstep this line of behavior that is considered by God to be wrong, then He will reveal more and more things that He would like to change in our lives. As we continue to adopt these revelations of God's will for us, we will find ourselves farther and farther from the original line (which is to not indulge in our addiction). Eventually, we will find ourselves so far from our original line in the sand, so to speak, that even when we have a bad day, the thought of using or engaging in our addiction is not even a remote possibility. This is a joyous place to be.

To this end, we see that all who want to be unanimously reformed in their lives must accept Jesus Christ's offer for Salvation first and foremost. Then, they must draw a line and say, "If God is against it, so am I!"

Step #2
EVERY SIN HAS ITS ORIGIN IN OUR HEARTS

Before I came to Christ, I tried to overcome my addictions over and over again through regular attendance at group meetings in society. I would spend hours upon hours sulking in my coffee, smoking cigarettes, and discussing my endless desire to drink. Sound familiar? Why didn't this type of activity help me?

Ephesians 5:11-12 reminds us to *"have no fellowship with the unfruitful works of darkness, but rather reprove them. For it is a shame even to speak of those things which are done of them in secret."* Our sins of the past must be forgotten. To meditate and discuss them openly only gives place to the devil. I decided a long time ago I would rather tell people what God has done for me than to tell people what I had done to God.

Constant meditation (thinking) on our desire to fulfill a fleshly lust will ultimately lead to acting out our desire. If we're fortunate to avoid it physically, we will seldom avoid it mentally. *Proverbs 23:7* reads, *"For as he thinketh in his heart, so is he…"* For me to avoid the seemingly unending desire to fulfill my desire to feed my addiction, I needed to discipline myself to avoid talking about it (in a desirous way) and avoid thinking about it. By thinking about it, I was actually making it easy for myself to do wrong. *Romans 13:14* states, *"But put ye on the Lord Jesus Christ, and make not provision for the flesh, to fulfil the lusts thereof."*

I saw an old friend at a local grocery store. He had heard that I had stopped using drugs and had "found religion." I explained how Jesus had changed my life and given me power over my addictions to both drugs and alcohol. He exclaimed his gladness and went on to tell me that he had been sober for three weeks. He had finally quit his job that led to after-hours drinking and had moved out of his buddy's house (who liked to have drinking parties regularly). Realizing these were both good first steps, I encouraged him to visit church and offered to pick him up. He gave me the address. Unfortunately, the young man had chosen to take up residence in an apartment that was directly adjacent to a popular bar in town. He never made it to church. Why did this man fail in his recovery? He made it easy for himself to do wrong. Even if he never left his house, the constant sounds of the music in the bar beneath him would never let the thought of drinking leave his mind!!

You see, the heart can accustom itself to sin. An act that once would seem terrible and undeniably wrong can, by contemplating it too often, become attractive. *Proverbs 4:23* reads, *"Keep thy heart with all diligence; for out of it are the issues of life."* Everything I ever searched for in life – the important issues of life: Love,

Joy, Peace, Happiness, Friendship, Financial Freedom – were always withheld from me during my times of addiction. Why was that? Because the important issues of life are given by God, and He never entrusts them to those who do not work hard (diligent) to keep (guard) their hearts from being hardened from the deceitfulness of sin.

REMEMBER: Before you ever did it, you thought about it!!

Step #3
IT IS EASIER TO KEEP THE HEART CLEAN THAN TO CLEAN IT AFTER IT HAS BEEN DEFILED.

Oh, what a truth this is! When my wife and I were first married, I had quite a few lessons to learn. I was a 28-year-old bachelor and was not accustomed to cleaning up after myself. My favorite meal was chili-n-fries surprise (the recipe is available for a small charge). My wife refused to cook it because of the extreme mess that the grease and chili sauce would make on her white stove. I was forced to suffer. However, a friend of my wife's asked her to work a few hours every Monday afternoon at her beauty supply store. She consented, and I was left to fend for myself in order to obtain dinner on Monday nights. Praise the Lord, chili-n-fries surprise! In my desire to consume this long-awaited meal, I overlooked the cleaning of the stove. When the next Monday rolled around, I found the chili sauce and grease stains from the previous week's delicatessen still splattered on my wife's stove. It was gross, and there was no way I could prepare a meal on this filth. When my wife arrived home later that evening, I asked her when she was planning on the cleaning the stove. BIG MISTAKE. Our first fight. I learned a valuable lesson that night. After an hour of scrubbing, I learned it is easier to keep a kitchen stove clean than to clean it after it has been stained.

This is the same truth we are taught in the Bible. Over and over again we are faced with examples of people who chose to associate with sin with hopes that it would not lead them to a sinful condition. Lot was a righteous man *(II Peter 2:8)* yet he chose to associate with ungodly men *(Psalm 1:1)*, he had day to day contact with sin *(Psalm 1:1)*,and he allowed the people around him to decay into moral wickedness with no good use for God *(Psalm 1:1)*. Yes, Lot's life was ultimately spared by God. However, He in no way prospered terrible sins *(Genesis 19)*. How can this mistake be avoided in your life? Follow these three simple verses:

Proverbs 22:3 – "A prudent man foreseeth the evil, and hideth himself: but the simple pass on, and are punished."

Proverbs 6:27-28 – "Can a man take fire in his bosom, and his clothes not be burned? Can one go upon hot coals, and his feet not be burned?"

Remember: If you do what you've always done, then you will be what you've always been.

Proverbs 4:23 – "Keep thy heart with all diligence; for out of it are the issues of life."

Step #4
WE CANNOT FIGHT A FLESHLY APPETITE BY INDULGING IN IT

Disregarding this principle has caused such great pain and failure for many years. It is also this very same principle that God will bring to our remembrance every time we feel like indulging in any fleshly desires. This principle has done more to discourage the desire to wander than any of the others.

If the truth be known, the failure to recognize and apply this principle to our lives is usually at the core of every besetting sin.

An appetite is a dangerous thing. If disciplined, it can be controlled. If not, it can control an individual. God has given within each of His children a power to control our appetites. The need for food, drink, and sexual satisfaction are all God-given, legitimate needs. However, Satan will twist them into lusts which, when coupled with enticement, lead to a life of sin and Spiritual and sometimes physical death. *James 1:14-16* says, *"But every man is tempted, when he is drawn away of his own lust, and enticed. Then when lust hath conceived, it bringeth forth sin: and sin, when it is finished, bringeth forth death. Do not err, my beloved brethren."*

Remember the old commercial that advertised KOOL cigarettes? The ad (falsely) stated that "They Satisfy." Well, if this were true, then we could all smoke one KOOL cigarette and our appetite would be satisfied, and we would never need to indulge that appetite again. The appetite created with indulgence will only intensify. Indulging in any fleshly appetite only makes it stronger, never weaker.

Not too long ago, I listened to a documentary on starving children in the third world. My heart was broken as the narrator explained that though the children were starving, they do not feel the hunger pains that we feel right before dinnertime. Rather, they have suppressed their appetite for so long that their starvation is not accompanied with the pain of hunger.

It is the same way with any fleshly desire that we struggle with. Whether it be cigarettes, drugs, alcohol, overeating, adulterous thoughts, pornography, gambling, or any other crippling appetite, if we do not feed it, do not give into it, it will die. The only way to destroy the appetite is to starve it. That is a promise from God.

So, the next time you feel that urge to indulge in a sinful, fleshly desire, resign yourself to just "skip that meal." When you skip a meal, you will see that after a few minutes or hours you have lost your appetite for that meal. You may not skip every meal, but eventually your desire will starve itself to death, and the hunger will be gone. Don't let the devil tell you if you have just one more cigarette, just one more drink, or just one more chocolate bar you will be satisfied.

Ecclesiastes 5:10 – "He that loveth silver shall not be satisfied with silver; nor he that loveth abundance with increase: this is also vanity."

Step #5
SMALL COMPROMISES LEAD TO GREAT DISASTERS
(Otherwise known as little sins lead to big sins.)

So many students and friends of the ministry have asked me questions like this:

"Brother Steve, I have stayed away from my old friends. I have stopped acting the way I used to. I go to church at least once a week, but I still ended up engaging in my addiction. Why doesn't this work?"

Such a difficult question to the student but such an easy answer from God.

I will usually ask them where they are in their Bible reading, Scripture memory, prayer life, mid-week service attendance, witnessing, and what they are doing for service to the Kingdom (bus route, cleaning church, nursery work, helping others, etc.). Without fail, they have fallen away for only two to three weeks… then bang! The devil acquires a foot hold.

How does this happen? Well, here is God's easy answer: *Luke 16:10 – "He that is faithful in that which is least is faithful also in much: and he that is unjust in the least is unjust also in much."* God says if we are consistent (faithful) in all the little things (questions asked earlier); we will be consistent (faithful) in the big things (remaining victorious). However, if inconsistent in the little things, we will fail in the big things. The reason is simple: God loves the little things. You see, this list of small things determines your master. You cannot serve God and earthly lusts. *Matthew 6:24* says, *"No man can serve two masters: for either he will hate the one, and love the other; or else he will hold to the one, and despise the other. Ye cannot serve God and mammon."* You will have no choice but to love one and hate the other. The more you do for God, the more you will learn to love Him. Why do we love Him? Because He first loved us!

Remember this: Small compromises lead to great disasters. You may compromise your Bible reading, church attendance, or service requirements now, but the consequences are guaranteed to be great. If you are not yielding yourself to the little requests of God, you will yield yourself to the little requests of the enemy. And, him alone will you serve. *Romans 6:16* says, *"Know ye not, that to whom ye yield yourselves servants to obey, his servants ye are to whom ye obey; whether of sin unto death, or of obedience unto righteousness?"*

Commit today to do the little things every day. **You will never read your Bible every day until you read your Bible on the days you don't want to.**

Step #6
THOSE WHO DO NOT LOVE THE LORD WILL NOT HELP US SERVE THE LORD

John 15:19 says, *"If ye were of the world, the world would love his own: but because ye are not of the world, but I have chosen you out of the world, therefore the world hateth you."*

Will my friends want anything to do with me now that I am a Christian? That was the question I asked after I gave my life to Jesus. It wasn't long before I found the answer. If I acted like them, they would accept me. When I acted like Christ, they rejected me.

I struggled to determine the correct path. You see, I wanted Christ in my life, but I also wanted Christ in my friends' lives. If I broke my ties with my worldly friends, they would lose their opportunity to learn of Christ. So, I tried to live as a child of God while hanging out with the devil's kids. As you would expect, more often than not, they would tempt me to do things that I did not want to do anymore. Eventually, I would give in.

It was at this time God showed me why misery loves company. You see, if I lived right and remained right, my old friends would feel guilt and shame for their behavior. But, if I lived wrong, they would prove that Christ has no affect on a person's life. The guilt for their lifestyle would be removed. They would lay the snare (temptation) and wait for me to fall. *Proverbs 24:15* says, *"Lay not wait, O wicked man, against the dwelling of the righteous; spoil not his resting place:"* They would work hard to lure me back into the world. They wanted to see that the Christian life does not work!

I found that when I got right and stayed right, they went left. However, when the law of sowing and reaping would kick in and they would find themselves at the bottom, they would not look to their friends who did the things they did. Rather, they called on me. They would ask me what I did to change my life because my change was real. Others were not. What a blessing! I have been able to counsel with literally dozens of friends from the past, in God's timing, and tell them that Christ died for their sins. It has also led to prosperity in my Christian life and blessed happiness. Just like the Bible promises in *Psalm 1:1-3* – *"Blessed is the man that walketh not in the counsel of the ungodly, nor standeth in the way of sinners, nor sitteth in the seat of the scornful. But his delight is in the law of the LORD; and in his law doth he meditate day and night. And he shall be like a tree planted by the rivers of water, that bringeth forth his fruit in his season; his leaf also shall not wither; and whatsoever he doeth shall prosper."*

Don't forget it – THOSE WHO DO NOT LOVE THE LORD WILL NOT HELP YOU SERVE THE LORD!

Step #7
OUR SINFUL HABITS DO HURT THOSE WHO FOLLOW US

Have you ever wondered if anybody cared? Have you ever thought about trying something drastic to get yourself noticed? *"Maybe then they would know I needed their help,"* you might say.

One of the lies from the father of lies (the devil) is that no one is watching or caring so no one is affected by our behavior. Since the dawn of time, the devil has deceived us into believing that our behavior will only affect, hurt, or damage ourselves. He did it in the beginning with Eve. Little did she know that her sin would then be shared by her husband, which, in turn, would lead to the fall of man and woman. Little did she know that a curse would be placed on herself and her husband and all generations to follow.

The devil deceived in the life of Lot. Not realizing that having day-to-day contact with sinners was damaging to his family, he stubbornly left his homeland. His lack of leadership over his family led to the death of his wife and uncontrolled behaviors by his daughters and himself.

The devil deceived in the life of David. Little did David know that if he stayed home from battle (where he belonged at the time), he would suffer a temptation that would lead to adultery. The consequences would be a woman would lose her husband to a plot of murder, and her son would die as a newborn infant. Over and over again in Scripture we see that sinful behavior has a profound effect on those who follow us.

Who, pray tell, are the ones who follow you? That is simple: Those whose lives are spent in relationship with yours. If you were to die today, would you have 100 people at your funeral? Most people would like to think so. How about 50? Or 35? Or 20? How about one? Would you have at least one person at your funeral? Yes, I believe we would all have at least one and probably closer to 100. Well, whether they actually say it to you or not, those are the people you hurt with your behavior. Those are the people affected by your sinful habit. They may not feel the pain you feel, but they feel pain. They may not say the things to you that you need said to help you, but they think them and wish they could find the courage to say them.

Romans 14:7 says, *"For none of us liveth to himself, and no man dieth to himself."* Your life affects others the same way your death would affect others. Choose today to let your life have a profound effect of good on others. No matter the cost. No matter the sacrifice. Make the choice. Today and tomorrow and onward from this point, your good habits will help those who follow you. Choose today to be a regular learner at church. Choose to read your Bible verses that will help you overcome. Choose today to be helpful to those who come to Reformers Unanimous. Choose today to make a difference in the lives of your congregation, the lives of your community, and a difference in the Kingdom of God.

Step #8
IT IS NOT POSSIBLE TO FIGHT A FLESHLY TEMPTATION WITH FLESHLY WEAPONS

Oh, so many times we have lost students either temporarily or permanently because they believed the lie of the devil that the world had something to offer their recovery. Whether it be the patch, secular counseling, evaluation of childhood, methadone, Prozac, or any other fleshly (worldly) weapon that is intended to curb our stubborn habits and inappropriate behavior, it will not (WILL NOT!) cure us of our affliction. Praise God, the battle is inside of us and that is exactly where Christ has chosen to take up residence in our lives! You see, the battle cannot be won with a fleshly (worldly) weapon because the battle is Spiritual. *II Corinthians 10:3-5* says, *"For though we walk in the flesh, we do not war after the flesh: (For the weapons of our warfare are not carnal, but mighty through God to the pulling down of strong holds;) Casting down imaginations, and every high thing that exalteth itself against the knowledge of God, and bringing into captivity every thought to the obedience of Christ;"*

It is simple to believe but hard to apply. Whenever we have a stubborn thought, we must cast it down. Remember, as a man thinks in his heart, so is he. Principle #2 says every sin has its origin in our hearts. It is our responsibility to protect our hearts with all diligence because out of the heart are the very most important issues in life. If there is going to be any good or anything worth commending come out of our lives, we must first concentrate on things that are true, honest, just, lovely, pure, and of a good report. *Philippians 4:8* says, *"Finally, brethren, whatsoever things are true, whatsoever things are honest, whatsoever things are just, whatsoever things are pure, whatsoever things are lovely, whatsoever things are of good report; if there be any virtue, and if there be any praise, think on these things."* To avoid a habitual action or reaction to your negative thoughts, you must cast down the thought and bring your mind under subjection to the obedience of Christ. You will have a lot of help with this, you see, because I John 4:4 says, *"Ye are of God, little children, and have overcome them: **because greater is he that is in you, than he that is in the world.**"*

The world has nothing to offer you in your quest for recovery. You can believe what you are reading or you can try the world yourself. But, with Christ, all things are possible if you only believe.

Step #9
WE LOSE OUR FREEDOM TO CHOOSE WHEN WE GIVE IN TO TEMPTATION AND...OUR CONSEQUENCES ARE INEVITABLE AND INCALCULABLE AND UP TO GOD

When we first take hold of a vice, it is extremely pleasurable. At times it may seem to be the only time we feel happy, and the only time we experience any comfort in our lives. However, the Bible warns in *Proverbs 20:17*, *"Bread of deceit is sweet to a man; but afterwards his mouth shall be filled with gravel."* You can clearly see that while deceitful and wrong actions may bring temporary pleasure, afterwards it leaves a very bad taste in your mouth. The consequences for your behavior then belong to God. *Proverbs 9:17-18* says, *"Stolen waters are sweet, and bread eaten in secret is pleasant. But he knoweth not that the dead are there; and that her guests are in the depths of hell."* No matter how much enjoyment we may receive from our stubborn habits or addictions, we can be sure that the consequences are never worth it.

We must realize that God is watching us. He watches every single thing we do. *Proverbs 5:21* says, *"For the ways of man are before the eyes of the LORD, and he pondereth all his goings."* The word ***"pondereth"*** means to weigh or consider. What does He consider? He considers the proper actions that should be taken against our behavior to bring a proper reaction from us. His desire is for a repentance and a dependence on Him rather than on some vice that only brings temporal advice. Look at the warning that is given in the very next verse. Ask yourself if you are in this position. *Proverbs 5:22 says, "His own iniquities shall take the wicked himself, and he shall be holden with the cords of his sins."* This verse clearly indicates that once we grab hold of a wicked vice, it will begin to wrap itself around us. Though, at the beginning we may be able to get out of its hold, eventually, the cord will be tightened around us, and we will be held in bondage with the cords of our sin. Oh, that is what happened to me! Next is the important warning to those of us who struggle to fight back. The next verse – *Proverbs 5:23* – says, *"He shall die without instruction; and in the greatness of his folly he shall go astray."* This consequence (going astray, which leads to a premature physical and Spiritual death) cannot be monitored by us. It is determined by God. Until that unfortunate time that we experience this untimely demise, we will live among consequences that are designed to bring us back to God. The cure…very simple. *Isaiah 55:7* – the **Reformers Key Verse** – **"Let the wicked forsake his way, and the unrighteous man his thoughts: and let him return unto the LORD, and he will have mercy upon him; and to our God, for he will abundantly pardon."** We need God's mercy (not getting what we deserve). We need God's pardon (penalty removed for what we have done) so that we may start over. That is accomplished by simply turning from our way of doing things and from our way of thinking and returning to the Lord. **Reformers Unanimous is here to show you** how to do this. I hope you listen to what God has to say to you.

Step #10
GOD BALANCES GUILT WITH BLAME. ACCEPT THE BLAME FOR YOUR ACTIONS AND GOD WILL REMOVE THE GUILT

As a young man trying to get away from the strongholds of my addiction, I sought the counsel and help of people in the secular programs. Time and time again, they searched for hidden meaning in my behavior. They explained how my rebellion and desire to please myself was most assuredly to be blamed on my parents. They said that I had been forced into my sin by what they referred to as "bad surroundings." Many in society today are teaching us to shift the blame for our shortcomings on our parents, our upbringing, our economic background, our race, our minority status, and many other things. By shifting the blame to others, it temporarily removes the guilt.

You see, God designed us with a Spiritual equilibrium. When we commit sin, we experience guilt, and it throws our Spirit off-balance with our emotions. When society teaches us to shift the blame (or if we naturally shift the blame), we actually can circumvent that off-balance feeling of guilt temporarily. However, when the sin returns, the guilt is so much worse. Our feelings of failure increase to even higher levels. God's design is to administer guilt through His Spirit that lives within the believer. That guilt needs to be released, and God designed a formula for that to happen. It is found in *I John 1:9 – "If we confess our sins, he is faithful and just to forgive us our sins, and to cleanse us from all unrighteousness."* What a beautiful promise! **If** – A BIG WORD! If we do, He will. If we don't, He won't! If we confess (proclaim to God) our sin, He is faithful (for sure, 100% of the time, over and over again) to forgive (full pardon) our sins. He does not stop there. You see, we have been pardoned for our wrongdoing, but we are not cleansed from it. We still have the guilty feeling. We must be cleansed of all unrighteousness. If my daughter got dressed for Sunday school and then went outside and fell in the mud, I would not only forgive her for playing outside when it was raining and she was dressed for Sunday school, I would also clean her up. I would give her a bath and all new clothes? Why? Because when I bring her to Sunday school, I don't want anyone to know that she fell in the mud! That is what God wants to do for us. He wants to give us a full pardon for everything we have done in the past, and He wants to clean us up and put us in a new set of clothes. And, He is faithful! That means He wants to do this every time we sin against Him. He loves us that much. So, today, accept the blame for what you have done in your life. Confess it to God, and He will clean you up. Praise God!

We also teach you to periodically analyze your actions and reactions for which there are nine analyses:

1. When faced with another's need, do I respond in love? This is the willing sacrificial giving of one's self for the benefit of others without thought of return or self love. Or, do I respond in hate? This is the willing or unwilling giving of one's self to benefit others with selfish thoughts of return.

2. In the midst of difficult circumstances, do I respond in joy? This is a cheerful, calm delight in all the circumstances of life. Or, do I respond in frustration? This is a rejection or unhappy refusal in life's circumstances.

3. When uncomfortable situations arise, do I respond in peace? This is to be safe from harm in spirit, mind and body. Or, do I respond with worry? This is to live in fear of harm in spirit, mind and body.

4. When faced with the weakness of another, do I respond in longsuffering? This is an enduring temperament that expresses itself in patience with the shortcomings of others. Or, do I respond with a quick temper? This is irritability that negatively excites the passions.

5. When disappointed with someone, do I respond in gentleness? This is softness in manners. Or, do I respond in harshness? This is roughness in manners, temper or words.

6. When prompted to give toward a need, do I respond in goodness? This is conforming my life and conversations to behave benevolently towards others. Or, do I respond in meanness? This is refusal to be liberal with charity, thus, avoiding any personal expense.

7. When my beliefs are challenged by circumstances, do I respond in faith? This is personal measurement of the level of confidence in what Jesus Christ has done and will do in, through and for us. Or, do I respond in doubt? This is an attitude of unbelief that is characterized by rebellion and disobedience toward our Heavenly Father.

8. When faced with conflicts by others, do I respond in meekness? This is the ability for God's people to negotiate among others without causing friction. Or, do I respond in discord? This is any disagreement that produces angry passions, contests, disputes, litigations or war.

9. When given an opportunity to indulge in appetite, do I respond in temperance? This is being spirit controlled in all of life's pleasures. Or, do I respond in self-indulgence? This is self-control that ceases to control itself.

We ask you here at Reformers Unanimous to open your mind and heart to the following pages. For on these pages are words that will guide you to the Truth and teach you how to walk in that Truth. As you believe in the Truth and walk in the Truth, you will be completely free from dependency on alcohol, addictive drugs or any other destructive behavior.

Please! Trust these words for they are based on the Truth, the reality of all things, which is the Lord Jesus Christ. Through this program, thousands have been guided to the freedom you so desire.

Chapter 2

Freedom, Not Sobriety, is the Goal

*F*OR CENTURIES, THE FUNDAMENTAL belief held across most civilized cultures was that alcoholism, drug addiction and other destructive behaviors were a moral failing; a spiritual problem. Those who drank alcohol or partook in drugs and other destructive behavior were generally shunned in society. Alcoholics were, and in large part remain, objects of scorn. Much of the world still labors under these concepts. In 1874 Benjamin Rush first described alcoholism as a disease. In 1935 two individuals set about to create a fellowship where alcoholics could support each other in recovery. Primarily interested in keeping their own sobriety going and helping others do the same, Bill Wilson and Robert Smith, M.D. co-founded *Alcoholics Anonymous*, or better known as *AA*. Wilson and Smith's novel concept was the biological aspect of alcoholism. They described alcoholism as an allergy of the body. One of their first successes was to change the prevalent view of alcoholism from a moralistic, spiritual failing to a medical illness. Just as people were not responsible from a moral standpoint for contracting tuberculosis or cancer, neither were they morally responsible for their alcoholism. In 1956 the American Medical Association (AMA) named alcoholism as a disease. Throughout the world today, the existing, primary thought process regarding alcoholism and addiction is not only that they are diseases but that they are incurable diseases. We are told that even if we were to stop abusing substances, the disease would continue and that we would be alcoholics and addicts forever. It is this belief that is primarily responsible for the stagnation that has existed for the past 70 years or so in the treatment of addictive behaviors. It is this process that has given birth to the following two terrible and untrue slogans: **"ONCE AN ALCOHOLIC OR ADDICT, ALWAYS AN ALCOHOLIC OR ADDICT"** and **"RELAPSE IS PART OF RECOVERY."**

It is our intention here at Reformers Unanimous to change that thought process that has infiltrated the world and more than likely infiltrated your belief system. We ask you to now take your turn to end your existing thought pattern about alcoholism and addiction. Our belief at Reformers Unanimous is that you are NOT an alcoholic or an addict. Here at Reformers Unanimous, you are NOT an incurable disease. You have become dependent on substances or destructive behavior to cope with underlying conditions that you, through the guidance of Reformers Unanimous, are now going to reveal and heal through believing on and walking in the Truth. Thus, your dependency upon those substances and destructive behaviors will cease. We at Reformers Unanimous know that you are searching for help and that you have suffered great hopelessness and despair. You truly feel that there is no hope. Please, know that alcoholism and addiction are not diseases, but they are a lifestyle that you have chosen in response to certain underlying conditions in your life. As a minister of the Gospel of Jesus Christ and the Reformers Unanimous International Director for the past eight years (Ben Burks) and as an Internal Medicine physician with a specialty in Addiction Medicine (Dr. George Crabb), we can write with complete certainty that alcoholism, drug addiction and destructive behaviors are NOT diseases! Alcohol and drugs are not the problem. They are what you are using to help yourself cope with problems. Those problems always have physical, psychological and spiritual components, which can be anything from anemia, hypothyroidism, bi-polar disorder, deep emotional pain from past traumas, spiritual unfaithfulness and even spiritual death. But, foundational to them all is this: **WHEN THE UNDERLYING PROBLEMS ARE DISCOVERED AND DEALT WITH ACCORDING TO THE TRUTH, THE NEED FOR THE ALCOHOL, THE NEED FOR THE DRUGS AND THE NEED FOR THE DESTRUCTIVE BEHAVIOR DISAPPEARS.**

As you work through the Reformers Unanimous curriculum, it will help you discover what these problems are. For most, it is just not one problem but many, and all of them have the answer in the Truth. Reformers Unanimous will again help you identify these problems, acknowledge and handle these problems and heal these problems through the administration of the Truth.

All that has happened to you is that you have become dependent on alcohol, drugs or destructive behavior to cope with your underlying conditions. Alcohol, drugs and destructive behaviors are just a quick and easy way to change ordinary, everyday reality from unbearable to bearable. All it takes is a quick trip to the liquor store and a few drinks, a quick trip to the medicine cabinet and a few pills swallowed down the throat or a quick trip to the bedroom where a magazine is obtained from underneath the mattress and a few obscene pictures are looked at and instantaneous relief.

A young woman came to Reformers Unanimous from a southern state with a severe drinking problem. While she was in the Women's Discipleship Home, she found that one of her needs was to receive the Truth – Jesus Christ as her Savior. As she received Jesus Christ as her Savior and the Holy Spirit of God came into her life, He began to reveal to her certain things that had transpired when she was a little girl. Through group counseling as well as individual counseling with trained RU personal, she was able to remember a time of sexual molestation between her and an older cousin. Because of these strange and demeaning sexual practices he procured upon her, her self-esteem had been trampled. She had become demoralized and humiliated, and she did not know what to do about it. Thus, she started to drink. Yes, even though the drinking was minimal to begin with, it became heavier and harder as time went on. As she recalled these events and as she learned to walk in the Truth, which is the core curriculum of Reformers Unanimous, she was able to uncover the cause of her misery and shame. She also was able to find the courage in her newfound Savior Who liberated her from her past. This allowed her to walk in freedom, of which she is still doing today.

If we were to create a word in Reformers Unanimous that more accurately describes alcoholism, addiction or destructive behavior, the word would be "BONDAGITIS." I know this word bondagitis sounds crazy in place of alcoholism, drug addiction or self-destructive behavior, but we believe it portrays a more accurate vision of what is going on. Instead of saying, "I am an alcoholic" or "I am an addict," you would say, "I have bondagitis." You can't catch bondagitis; you cannot give bondagitis. You can, however, get rid of bondagitis. Bondagitis can be to alcohol, addictive street drugs, addictive prescription drugs or other destructive behaviors. What applies to drug and alcohol bondagitis applies to other bondagitis' as well. As you continue to read this book, we pray that you will open your mind and see where your bondagitis lies. Please, realize this. All bondagitis is a symptom and not the problem. As you work with the Reformers Unanimous Program, whether it be in one of the

Discipleship Homes in Rockford, Illinois or in one of the more than 700 local chapters across the world, you will find your healing of your bondagitis and be free from what has been tormenting you for so many years.

Most individuals that have been treated at other facilities were being treated as if the alcoholism, drug addiction and/or destructive behaviors were the problems when they were only symptoms of the problems. At Reformers Unanimous with its organized, structured curriculum that is based on the Truth, we help you uncover the "why" behind your addictive behaviors and set you on a new course with the Truth and in the Truth.

Before we progress more into the Reformers Unanimous Program, it is important for us to establish some basic physiological understanding in regards to dependence, tolerance and withdrawal. First, through prolonged use of certain drugs that have addictive qualities, we can develop a dependency on those drugs. Among these are alcohol, nicotine, cocaine, heroin, amphetamines, prescription pain killers (Vicodin, Lortab, Ultram, etc.) and sedative hypnotics (Xanax, Valium). This dependence can also occur with destructive behaviors. Addiction is defined as the "compulsive, physiological need for and use of a habit-forming substance or behavior." Addiction is characterized by tolerance and well-defined physiological symptoms upon withdrawal. All addictive drugs and destructive behaviors produce a reward system in the brain. This reward system is called the "meso-cortico-limbic dopamine system." Using addictive drugs or participating in destructive behavior gives us a sense of well being and alleviates bad feelings. After using a drug for a period of time or participating in destructive behavior, users frequently develop a tolerance for the drug or behavior. They need more of the substance (behavior) to accomplish the same feeling as when they began using the substance (behavior). For example, when we drink a can of regular soda, our blood sugar goes up and our pancreas releases insulin to help metabolize the carbohydrate (sugar) and balance out glucose levels. By a similar process, if we take a stimulant like methamphetamine, our body will counteract that change by producing sedative-like chemicals to return us to normal. However, as our body gets better and better at counteracting the disruptive effects of a drug such as methamphetamine, we experience less and less of the drugs effects because our body is learning how to cancel out a great deal of those effects. The problem is users don't typically say, at that point, "Well, the drug isn't doing much for me anymore, so I will just stop." Instead, they take increasingly larger or more frequent doses to produce the same relief from the underlying problems. That process just described is tragic! When you put a substance in your body that pushes it outside its range of peak function, your body learns to counteract the damage, and you must take more and more to get close to the original high. This, of course, escalates into a terrible race with yourself. If this race continues long enough, your body commits to a desperate act of self-protection. It will get "used to" the drug. That is, it will shift from normal functioning to a new level of tolerance or dysfunction. The moment your body becomes accustomed to life with the drug, the lack of it is going to be felt as a disruption or as abnormal. So, if you don't get the drug, you will feel symptoms of withdrawal. Once you shift to this new level of tolerance, you will find yourself taking the substance just so you can avoid the withdrawal symptoms. Different addictive drugs have different withdrawal symptoms. They can include:

- Nausea
- Watery Eyes
- Dizziness
- Fainting
- Muscle Spasms
- Seizures
- Bone Aches
- Muscle Aches
- Headaches
- Intestinal Cramping
- Runny Nose
- Goosebumps
- Loss of Appetite
- Insomnia
- Sweating
- Hallucinations
- Irritability
- Diarrhea
- Tremors
- Panic Attacks
- Chills
- Paranoia

- Anger
- Convulsions
- Heart Palpitations
- Rapid Breathing
- Rapid Heat Rate
- Apathy (lack of energy)
- Delirium
- Pain
- Depression
- Disorientation
- Fatigue
- Excess Periods of Sleep or even Psychosis (a mental state in which a person loses contact with reality)
- Death (i.e., alcohol withdrawal)

The length of time it takes to become dependent to the point of experiencing withdrawal upon abstinence is different for each drug and for each person taking the drug. A few weeks of abstinence from the drug is usually enough for the withdrawal symptoms to pass. But, after the withdrawal symptoms end, an individual will experience a return of the symptoms of the underlying condition for which the drug was initially taken to mask. If those underlying conditions are not treated, the return of these symptoms may cause so much discomfort again, the person will go back to using alcohol, addictive drugs and destructive behavior to obtain relief. This is the primary reason there is such a high level of relapse among people who have become dependent on alcohol, drugs and destructive behaviors. It has little to do with alcohol, drugs and destructive behaviors themselves and everything to do with the original causes that created the bondagitis.

In addition to physical dependence, we can develop psychological dependence. Psychological need is the perceived need to use a substance to cope with unpleasant feelings, such as:

- Depression
- Anxiety
- Stress
- Fear
- Uncertainty
- Frustration and the like

Relief from something unpleasant is a kind of reward called "negative reinforcement." This cycle is worsened by both the physical and psychological discomforts felt during abstinence. When we stop using the addictive drugs, alcohol or stop participating in the destructive behaviors that we have been using or performing to cope with unpleasant feelings, these feelings return as does the strong desire to return to the substances or behaviors that enabled us to cope with them in the first place. This is what characterizes psychological dependence.

Now, some people are able to break free from addictive substances and destructive behaviors, but they still exhibit the traits of someone that is dependent. You may have heard the term "dry drunk." This means that someone is no longer abusing and using but is still displaying the characteristics of an alcoholic or a drug addict. Some of these characteristics are:

- Insomnia
- Irritability
- Lying
- Denial About His or Her Condition
- Isolation
- Low Self-Esteem
- Displaying Immaturity, Insecurity and Anxiety

The above are some of the symptoms we see at Reformers Unanimous when our students discontinue using drugs or alcohol. When you don't treat the real issues behind the bondagitis, you may see another "tale tall" symptom. You may end up trading one addiction for another. This is called substitutionary addiction and is what takes place when you give a heroin addict methadone. You switch from one addiction to another. No healing has occurred. No freedom is ever achieved. You will see some become workaholics. Others will develop a eating disorder or turn to gambling, shopping or sex. This is because, one way or another, our bodies are always seeking to let us know, through our behavior and our feelings, that something is wrong and needs to be healed. So, what is the solution to the vicious cycle of bondagitis? First, all health issues, including the most common ones such as anxiety and depression, have biochemical, physiological, psychological, and spiritual roots in addition to being caused by stressful conditions at home or in the work place. For example, anxiety can be a deficiency of vitamin B1 and magnesium or by hormone imbalances. Insomnia is often caused by a need for calcium, magnesium or potassium. Insomnia can also be caused by hypoglycemia, thyroid or adrenal problems. Fatigue and low energy can result from chronic viral infections, anemia, low endocrine function, low blood sugar, yeast infection, chemical sensitivity and improper digestion. Headaches and dizziness are often linked to liver toxicity, dehydration, blood sugar abnormalities, low thyroid function, high blood pressure or even food allergies. Depression can be due to hypothyroidism, adrenal dysfunction, nutritional deficiencies, blood sugar problems and food allergies. Depression can also result from medical illnesses such as a stroke, heart attack, cancer, Parkinson's disease and other hormonal disorders. It can also be caused by a serious loss, difficult relationship, financial problems or any stressful, unwelcome change.

What has to be called for is the objective assessment of one's functioning. One of the first actions we take at Reformers Unanimous is to ruthlessly scrutinize, always under a physician's supervision and care, the specific necessity of any mind-altering or mood-altering medications our students are taking. As soon as any non-essential medications are out of their system, the feelings they were trying to suppress with drug use usually emerge. When this happens, we can see what symptoms the student was masking with drugs, alcohol or destructive behaviors. We can then identify the real issues burdening them, and we can help them as we, again, introduce them to the Truth, which is Jesus Christ.

Any individual who has worked through the Reformers Unanimous curriculum and has walked out with complete recovery was not cured from alcoholism or addiction, but they were cured from the condition that was causing them to use alcohol, addictive drugs, or destructive behavior to make life bearable.

Identifying and then healing the underlying causes of bondagitis is all about restoring one's body, soul and spirit to their God-ordained balance. We are aware that a just balance is the desire of God, not only in business transaction but in a balanced life. Proverbs 16:11 says, *"A just weight and balance are the LORD's: all the weights of the bag are his work."* We find that false balances or an unbalanced life is detrimental. Proverbs 11:1 and 20:23 says, *"A false balance is abomination to the LORD: but a just weight is his delight." Divers weights are an abomination unto the LORD; and a false balance is not good."* One way or another, our bodies and our souls are always seeking to get back into that spirit-led balance. Whenever an imbalance is present in our physical, mental or emotional areas of life, it always manifests itself outwardly on the physical or emotional plain. This is how our bodies tell us that something is wrong. It is how we become aware of imbalances. Most of us are constantly modifying our moods and physical sensations with substances and behavior patterns. We wake up and feel a little groggy or slow, and we reach for a coffee. At the end of a meal, if we feel unsatisfied, we may have a sweet desert. If we feel a little stressed or depressed, we may have something to eat. If we feel a little out of sorts, we may go shopping. What is the goal of all those behavioral patterns? We are striving to achieve balance that God has ordained for our lives.

It is Reformers Unanimous' mission to help each student regain that balance between body, soul and spirit (the spirit being the foundation.) Here at Reformers Unanimous, we want and desire to teach the student how to obtain that balance without the use of substances. On the other hand, we are teaching them to correct whatever is causing the imbalance. Most of the time it is a lack of a salvation relationship with Jesus Christ as well as a lack of a dynamic, intimate, personal relationship with Jesus as their Savior and Friend.

We are going to cover a quick word on denial as we close out this chapter. Denial is obviously a strong emotion. You are out there right now struggling with alcohol, drug addiction or destructive behaviors. You are saying, "I can quit anytime I want to." Or, you are saying, "I am okay. I don't need to quit." We hear all these statements in the Reformers Unanimous Program as well as many more like-sounding statements. But, here is the truth my friend. You have been secretly trying to quit many times, haven't you? And, you failed! You know you need to quit but you cannot. This is why you are falling back on the above-stated phrases. You are very well aware of the truth – YOU NEED TO QUIT. But, we also know that you are afraid because you have lost control of yourself. We would like to, in the most gentle and compassionate way we can, make this statement to you. **WE KNOW YOU WOULD LIKE TO QUIT, AND WE KNOW YOU HAVE SO DESPERATELY TRIED IN THE PAST AND FAILED. BUT, MY FRIEND, WE HAVE FOUND SOMETHING THAT WORKS. IT IS THE TRUTH. IT IS JESUS!**

Chapter 3

Relapse is Not Part of Recovery

*A*GOVERNMENT STUDY OF MORE THAN 1.5 million drug and alcohol users found that more than twenty-five percent of heroin users had tried five or more treatment centers without success. The national relapse rate for all drugs is nearly eighty percent and even higher (eighty-six percent for users of alcohol and heroin). Most relapses occur within a few weeks of alcoholics or addicts attempting sobriety and many occur within a few days. Even people who have been sober for ten, twenty or even thirty years relapse. Most addicts and alcoholics relapse not just once but many times. No matter how desperately they want to quit, they repeatedly return to alcohol, addictive drugs or destructive behaviors of choice. Most of the treatment programs available in our society today are based on the twelve-step program of Alcoholics Anonymous (AA). The only requirement for AA membership is the desire to stop drinking, but it is not open to everyone. It is only open to individuals who will publicly declare themselves to be alcoholics or addicts and who are willing to give up their inerrant right of independence by declaring themselves powerless over addictive drugs and alcohol as stated in step one. Step one reads as follows: **WE ADMITTED WE WERE POWERLESS OVER ALCOHOL – THAT OUR LIVES HAD BECOME UNMANAGEABLE**. To give up our power to change for the better is inherently distasteful to everyone and to force people to affirm they are alcoholics or addicts so that they can speak in a meeting is demoralizing and shameful. Such declarations ruin a healthy self-image. They convince us that even though we obtain sobriety, we remain broken instead of whole and spoiled instead of fresh and new. Here at Reformers Unanimous, we believe that those who are reluctant to affirm that they are still addicts or alcoholics know, even if subconsciously, that the mental programming inerrant in proclaiming ones self to be an addict or alcoholic is hugely detrimental. In fact, there is a saying used in twelve-step programs and most treatment centers that says: **RELAPSE IS PART OF RECOVERY**. This is just another dangerous slogan that is based on a lie, and it only gives people permission to relapse because they think that when they do, they are on the road to recovery. Just because the failure rate of some treatment programs is so enormous does not mean that relapse has to be the norm. Relapse is NOT part of recovery but it is part of failure. Relapse is a return to bondagitis. You may now be starting to understand why the relapse rate is so high. It is because people are being programmed to relapse. They are trying to quit without curing the underlying causes.

When you look at the world-wide picture of relapse among alcoholics and addicts, it is hard to not understand the slogan that "RELAPSE IS PART OF RECOVERY." But, the success of the Reformers Unanimous Program has proven otherwise. We believe here at Reformers Unanimous that staying sober is a natural byproduct of walking in the Truth of Jesus Christ with the underlying conditions that were responsible for your bondagitis healed. Many of our graduates call us, write us and e-mail us rejoicing in their newfound liberty in Jesus Christ. And, without exception, they are free. When our students come to us, whether it be in the Discipleship Homes or in local chapters around the world, they come wiling to look deeply into their past and into the darkened recesses of their minds. This look inward is always filtered through the Word of God. With His love and compassion being the guide, our students become willing to look within for the reasons for their substance abuse or behavior, and they are then willing to submit themselves to the power of the indwelling Holy Spirit to make changes within themselves to achieve the goal of freedom. They give up trying to fix themselves and allow our Heavenly Father, through His indwelling Holy Spirit, to fix them. They give up blaming other people and circumstances for their conditions and take personal responsibility for their actions, both past and present as is reiterated in Principal #10 – GOD BALANCES GUILT WITH

BLAME. Accept the blame for your actions and God will remove the guilt. I John 1:9 says, *"If we confess our sins, he is faithful and just to forgive us our sins, and to cleanse us from all unrighteousness."*

An essential element to the recovery program at Reformers Unanimous is that the staff regards bondagitis as no more or no less than someone's effort to cope with the pain and frustration of life. This is how you should think of it as well. We know that you don't want to be a drunkard or hooked on addictive drugs. You do it because you can't cope with your life. You can't completely cope without the power of God in your life. We recognize here at Reformers Unanimous that you have used substances to try to regain your lost balance. We are aware that you use substances to alter your mood, to cover up your sadness, to ease your heartbreak, to lighten your stress load, to blur your painful memories, to escape your hurtful reality or to make your unbearable days and nights bearable. Nothing else has worked for you, has it? No doctor, therapist, treatment center, addiction specialist, parent, spouse, sibling or friend has provided you with a remedy for your problems and pain. But, you've found a remedy and it works! That's the problem with addictive drugs and alcohol. They work! They may work only temporarily, and they have terrible killing side effects. But, they do work! They provide release from the pain that drives you to use and abuse substances and behaviors. At Reformers Unanimous we have never found it to be otherwise. At the bottom of every person's bondage is pain. Discovering the pain and healing it in the light of God's Holy Word is the essential step in ending bondagitis. One of the toughest jobs we have here at Reformers Unanimous is to help our students unlearn what they have learned at other treatment centers. What you believe is one of the most important aspects of your recovery and of living a life of freedom in Jesus Christ.

What we want most for you at Reformers Unanimous is that you live your life in the freedom that Jesus Christ purchased for you when He died on the cross, when He was buried in the tomb for three days and when He rose victoriously on that third day. We desire for you to walk in that freedom being completely free of the need to use addictive substances or destructive behaviors. To accomplish this, you will be led through the Reformers Unanimous curriculum that will first introduce you to the Truth – THE LORD JESUS CHRIST. You must know for certain that Jesus Christ is your Savior and that you have placed your faith and trust in Him for your eternal security. Once this is established, the Reformers Unanimous curriculum will teach you how to walk in the Lord Jesus Christ. They will teach you how to walk in that Truth by teaching you the ten principles outlined earlier in this book and by periodically analyzing your actions and reactions to the nine specific areas we discussed briefly at the beginning of this book. You will be immersed in the Reformers Unanimous text book, "Nevertheless I Live," where you are taught about the crucified Christian life that is bedrock to a life of freedom. You will also be lead through the "Stronghold's" Discipleship Course and be instructed on how to daily journal your walk with God. This is why it is imperative for you to engage yourself at the Men or Women's Discipleship home in Rockford, Illinois, or engage yourself in one of the over 700 local chapters around this world where trained men and women can lead you through this God-ordained, Biblically-founded curriculum. It will take discipline and dedication as well as determination on your part. But, you have in front of you the answer to your bondage. Ninety-four percent of individuals who pick up the Reformers Unanimous curriculum trust the Lord Jesus Christ as their Savior and learn to walk in the Truth. REMEMBER: Failure will only come when you fail to follow the Truth.

Chapter 4
It Can Be You

WHAT YOU BELIEVE ABOUT yourself, alcoholism, addiction, and destructive behaviors as well as the Word of God and about the possibility of a recovery without relapse are key factors or beliefs in determining if you will overcome your bondagitis to addictive substances and behaviors. Some of your beliefs will be based on what you've experienced and heard about treatment for substance abuse. Perhaps you don't believe you can be helped. But, we, at Reformers Unanimous want to let you know that there is hope. In fact there is always hope for freedom. Perhaps you have heard that other dependent people have relapsed frequently, and, therefore, you have given yourself permission to relapse. You have convinced yourself that if a trigger presents itself, you must give in to that trigger. Perhaps none of the above applies to you, but you have been drinking or using addictive drugs for so long and have tried so many times to stop that you believe you can't be helped. Based on experiences like these, your doubts that a recovery without relapse is possible are understandable, but they are not accurate, healthy or correct. We here at Reformers Unanimous have written this book to let you know that recovery without relapse is totally possible through our Lord Jesus Christ. One of the strong beliefs that students have at Reformers Unanimous is that relapse seldom occurs among them. They believe that freedom is the norm. Among the people that have graduated from Reformers Unanimous, fewer than six percent have relapsed. This success rate is astronomically opposite of the national relapse rate, which as I mentioned before is eighty percent overall for drug users and eight-six percent for users of alcohol and heroin. So, my friend, you can be helped if you follow the Reformers Unanimous curriculum that leads you into the Truth. One of the most comforting and important messages we offer to those who contact us at Reformers Unanimous is that there is hope. We tell them that they can have recovery without relapse. They can be faced with triggers and they can properly respond to those triggers in a positive, healthy way.

For the remainder of this chapter, we need to look at the physiology behind triggering events, what a trigger event is and how we here at Reformers Unanimous go about submitting that triggering event to the indwelling Holy Spirit of God so that our recovery will remain free of relapse.

The subject of addiction and its triggers, along with its associated cravings and destructive behavior, are never easy to address. Addiction grieves the heart of God, does great damage to the individual, and without exception, affects others. We need to be clear on this subject of addiction and its triggers. There is no excuse for playing around with the triggers of our addiction. We must strip away any excuse for denial or reason we might use for justifying our casual attitude toward triggers and ultimate addictive behavior. Triggers are dealt with in the most serious manner here at Reformers Unanimous. Whether our addictions have to do with alcohol, drugs, food, sex, gambling, self-harm or shopping, the addictive behavior is always preceded by some triggering event that initiates thoughts, feelings, and sensations, leading to cravings to engage the addictive behavior. If not properly handled the craving will manifest itself in an outward act of destructive behavior.

The trigger, when nurtured, takes on a life of its own. The thought generated about engaging in the addictive behavior and the emotional reward resulting from the addictive behavior becomes a preoccupation. This preoccupation is so strong that it stimulates a craving to use. The craving is then accompanied by a response in the meso-cortico-limbic dopamine system in the brain with the resultant physiological response in the body. The meso-cortico-limbic dopamine system in our brain has been keenly conditioned to the euphoric feelings of previous addictive thought and behavior.

You see, the brain tissue of someone who is addicted eventually undergoes structural and functional changes. The triggering event leads to a thought that begins to "fire off" these euphoric memories, and if not properly dealt with, lead us into cravings. These physiological responses in the brain and body are both real and powerful. If these responses are not handled appropriately, they will lead to addictive behavior. A Biblical example illustrating a triggering event followed by destructive behavior is found in the life of Achan. The nation of Israel was to defeat the city of Jericho in their effort to conquer the land of Canaan. As they went through the city of Jericho, they were instructed to not take any of the material goods for themselves. All that was in the city of Jericho belonged to God. The instructions were given in plain and simple terms for all to understand. The material items were off limits. Here is where we find Achan exposed to a triggering event, which ultimately led to a thought, a craving, and finally an action that led to his destruction. First, we notice the triggering effect in Joshua 7:21 – "**When I saw among the spoils** a goodly Babylonish garment, and two hundred shekels of silver, and a wedge of gold of fifty shekels weight, then I coveted them, and took them; and, behold, they are hid in the earth in the midst of my tent, and the silver under it." This was the triggering event. He saw what was forbidden for him to possess. Instead of shutting the process down, he allowed a thought to be generated and that thought became a preoccupation which led to a craving. This is found in his statement in verse 21 – "**then I coveted**."

This triggered an emotion in his soul of covetousness. His meso-cortico-limbic dopamine system in his brain was "firing off" signals giving him a sense of euphoria and excitement if he could just take and possess these items. This set him up for the final phase, which is the performance of the addictive or destructive behavior. This is also found in his statement in verse 21 – "**and took them**." Achan obviously did not cast down this thought and subsequent craving. If not dealt with properly, one will always act on the trigger despite the known consequences. The consequences seem distant and unreal at this time, but as is normal after acting on a craving, shame, guilt and fear come flooding in. Achan, of course, did what was natural. He attempted to hide his activity from his authority. This is also found in verse 21, where he states, "**they are hid**." This is the downward spiral that many are repeating today in many treatment programs and that was seen in the life of Achan – "**...I saw...I coveted...I took...I hid.**" This is the way it happens! However, most fail to see the final phase of the progression – "I GOT CAUGHT!"

REMEMBER: We rarely think of getting caught before we indulge the addictive behavior. We think about it only after the excitement and euphoria wear off and the paranoia sets in. We can be incredibly inventive when it comes to rationalizing our addictive, destructive behavior. The heat of the moment, the excitement of the addictive behavior and the adventure and forbidden pleasure drive away all reason. We seek, we covet, we take and we hide.

An important part of recovery is being able to recognize our triggers and how cravings manifest in our body, brain and soul *(mind, will and emotion)*. God wants us to be aware of every thought and feeling that is associated with the triggering event. As we acknowledge our thoughts and emotions, we have a choice over our behavior. We can allow the triggering event to have control by allowing it to produce a thought and a craving, or we can submit to God and allow His Spirit to control our behavior.

Often, cravings are our longing for things to be different than the way they are in the moment. All addictions involve some form of fantasy. If an addiction does not divert a person's mind from reality, it is not worth doing. We must realize that life's stresses often feel overwhelming and unbearable. Fantasy is a method of survival that allows mental escape from the pressure and situation at hand. Fantasy creates excitement and anticipation, which in turn can trigger an addictive episode. Amnon illustrates this point of fantasy triggering a thought, a craving and subsequent destructive behavior. The triggering event is detailed for us in II Samuel 13:1-17. In these verses we find that Amnon had a beautiful half sister named Tamar. Both Amnon and Tamar had King David as their father but each had a different mother. Amnon was not satisfied with his current condition and wanted a relationship with Tamar. He fantasized over this non-existent relationship, and his mind became obsessed and preoccupied with it. For Amnon, seeing Tamar was a trigger that unleashed an incredible craving in the meso-cortico-limbic dopamine system of his brain to possess and control the desired object. In this case, the object was an individual, Tamar. However, in other cases it might be a drug, a bottle of liquor, pornographic material and the like. This trigger developed a violent lust for Tamar, which is seen in verse 2 of II Samuel 13 – *"And Amnon was so vexed, that he fell sick for his sister Tamar; for she was a virgin; and Amnon thought it hard for him to do any thing to her."* Another co-occurring trigger in Amnon's life is his friend, Jonadab. Jonadab helped facilitate making Amnon's fantasy a reality. An elaborate plan of deception was masterminded and implemented with the resulting fantasy becoming a reality in the sexual abuse of Tamar. In the midst of all this insanity, Tamar ushers forth words of reason in verses 12 and 13 – *"And she answered him, Nay, my brother, do not force me; for no such thing ought to be done in Israel: do not thou this folly. And I, whither shall I cause my shame to go? and as for thee, thou shalt be as one of the fools in Israel. Now therefore, I pray thee, speak unto the king; for he will not withhold me from thee."* But, with the craving in full force and dopamine flooding the pre-frontal cortex of the brain, reasonable thinking is easily pushed aside and dismissed by the addict. Amnon allows the trigger to produce a thought which generated an intense craving thus leading to the destructive behavior of sexually abusing his sister. After the conquest of the individual, or drug activity, our sense of reality and reason comes back. This, in turn, leads to tremendous feelings of guilt, shame and hatred toward the once-desired activity and anything associated with it. In the case of Amnon, it was Tamar. This is seen in the intense hatred Amnon manifested toward Tamar in verse 15 – *"Then Amnon hated her exceedingly; so that the hatred wherewith he hated her was greater than the love wherewith he had loved her. And Amnon said unto her, Arise, be gone."* Most often, the addict will have a loathsome attitude toward the addictive behavior after they have engaged in it. There is generally a deep disgust and intense hatred experienced by the addict. Amnon suffered the same.

Here at Reformers Unanimous we are not necessarily trying to get rid of or avoid these triggers in total because it is impossible. We live in a wicked world where unrighteous opportunities abound. We at Reformers Unanimous, instead, teach how to acknowledge the triggers and how to relate to them in a healthy, non-destructive, non-addictive way. Some will be faced with a trigger everyday of their life. Our desire at Reformers Unanimous is to educate the student so that they are aware of the emotions stimulated by the trigger and then taught to deal with such a trigger through righteous avenues. A prime example of facing a trigger daily is Joseph. In Genesis 39:7-12, the account is told of Joseph when he was in Egypt and in charge of Potiphar's house. Everything was at Joseph's disposal except Potiphar's wife. Joseph was in the midst of serving God wholeheartedly when he was faced with a trigger. The trigger he was facing was an invitation by Potiphar's wife to engage in an adulterous activity. This is seen in verse 7 – *"And it came to pass after these things, that his master's wife cast her eyes upon Joseph; and she said, Lie with me."* Joseph refused to allow the trigger to advance into a thought, craving, and subsequently to act upon it. Joseph does not allow the insane thinking of addictive, destructive behavior to set in, but he stays with a sane, rational and reasonable thought found in verses 8 and 9 – *"But he refused, and said unto his master's wife, Behold, my master wotteth not what is with me in the house, and he hath committed all that he hath to my hand; There is none greater in this house than I; neither hath he kept back any thing from me but thee, because thou art his wife: how then can I do this great wickedness, and sin against God?"* He expresses the cruel consequences that would be associated with his activity, including the broken bond of trust between him and Potiphar. But more importantly, he exposes the profound effect that this activity would have on his relationship with God (this is what we emphasize at Reformers Unanimous). Joseph indicates this effect in verse 9 – *"There is none greater in this house than I; neither hath he kept back any thing from me but thee, because thou art his wife: how then can I do this great wickedness, and sin against God?"*

Anytime we allow a trigger to produce a thought and then a craving leading to addictive activity it will affect our relationship with others and God. Now, this is only the beginning of the story when it comes to Joseph and his trigger. Many can extinguish a single trigger and many can do so out of their own gut wrenching self-effort. But, how about when your trigger keeps knocking on your door day after day? This is what happened with Joseph. The Bible indicates this in verse 10 – *"And it came to pass, as **she spake to Joseph day by day**, that he hearkened not unto her, to lie by her, or to be with her."* Joseph was confronted with this trigger every single day, and day by day he used the righteous reasoning spoken of above to eliminate the trigger and not allow it to germinate into a thought. As in many cases, the trigger can intensify, and this is exactly what we find happening in the life of Joseph. In verse 12 we see that Joseph was not only exposed to a verbal trigger but a physical one – *"And **she caught him by his garment**, saying, Lie with me: and he left his garment in her hand, and fled, and got him out."* This only makes the situation more intense. The intensity of the trigger makes Joseph go to his second line of defense. Not only did Joseph use his righteous reasoning, but he also used another means of escaping the trigger – HE RAN AWAY! Sometimes, when faced with the trigger, the only thing to do is run away. This is a sign of strength, not weakness. It is a strength to know your weaknesses. You should not only know your weaknesses but how to protect yourself from them. At Reformers Unanimous we assist the student in identifying their weaknesses and help them strategize a proper course of action to take when their weaknesses are exposed.

Triggers are things in the individual's daily life that tempts them to return to their addictive or

destructive behavior. They can take many forms from objects and smells to people and places. The first step is to identify the things in your life that make you want to get in a destructive pattern. Then, you should avoid these high-risk situations as much as possible. We must eliminate these things from our lives whenever we can. Here is the process that occurs:

TRIGGER > THOUGHT > CRAVING > ACTIVITY

The trigger, again, is someone, something or some situation that generates a thought about using. The thought in your head will start as an argument. You feel as though you are in a fight. Your body and brain are looking for an excuse to use again. It is vital to identify these thoughts and eliminate them as we will discuss later in this book. It takes effort to identify and stop a thought. However, allowing yourself to continue thinking about addictive, destructive behavior is choosing to do the addictive, destructive behavior. The further the thoughts are allowed to go, the craving from the meso-cortico-limbic dopamine system will become more real and intense and ultimately result in the addictive behavior. The only way to ensure that a thought won't lead to a craving and then the craving to an action is to stop the thought before it leads to a craving. Stopping the thought when it first begins prevents it from building into an overpowering craving. It is important to do it as soon as you realize that you are thinking about using.

At Reformers Unanimous we like to teach our students what triggers look like and how they potentially present themselves in everyday living. We have learned that the best way to defeat a trigger is to be prepared. The following is Reformers Unanimous' way of preparing the individual for the confrontation with triggers that will occur in their recovery without relapse.

When God made Adam and Eve, He placed them in a perfect environment. He gave them appetites. One such appetite was the desire for each other, and He wanted them to enjoy each other. Another was for food, and it was clear they could have at it except for one fruit, of course. A desire for Him was present, and He made sure He was always available for them at their request.

When man chose to disobey God's command, there were grave consequences. We are often reminded in the ten principles of RU, you can choose to do wrong, but you cannot choose the consequences. Perhaps the first sin was one of dissatisfaction. James, chapter one, tells us that the purpose temptation is allowed to come to us is to drive out the dissatisfaction in our lives to bring us to a position of "wanting nothing." God is not trying to give us satisfaction right now as much as He is trying to get us to rest in Christ so we will enjoy godliness with contentment.

When man and woman were removed from the garden, every appetite God had given them went with them.

However, now they are in a sinful environment as well as a sinful flesh, and man has been on one big binge ever since looking for satisfaction. Perhaps a fitting definition for addiction is any appetite on a binge.

Many appetites are actually good and Godly but taken in dissatisfaction is perhaps the root of many struggles. Learning those triggers that cause us discontentment are necessary to avoid the traps set to pull us back to living in the sinful flesh and not fulfilling the fruits of the Spirit.

TRIGGER EXAMPLES:

1. NEGATIVE THOUGHTS AND EMOTIONS

There is scientific research that shows a connection between negative emotions and relapse. Obviously, the Word of God has demonstrated this in many illustrations, but science will always fall in line with the Word of God. Certain negative thoughts and emotions can be sadness, guilt, anger, anxiety, rumination and "catastrophising." Something as simple as a news story about addiction can produce a thought and craving to return to the addictive behavior. Internal triggers such as negative emotions and thoughts are difficult to manage because they have no initial outward manifestation. Again, examples include getting angry over something that the addict believes justifies taking a drink, swallowing a pill or having an affair. It may be a blue or depressed mood that, through experience, the addict knows a couple lines of cocaine will alter the feeling into some perceived happiness no matter how short lived. Although feeling bad about one's self is frequently a constant companion of the student, he or she may use the internet to alter the feelings by talking to someone in a chat room and subsequently finding an anonymous, sexual partner no matter how unsafe such an adventure may be.

An illustration found in the Bible regarding a negative emotion leading to destructive behavior is in the life of Cain. In Genesis 4:4-5 we see that God had respect for Abel's offering but did not respect Cain's. *"And Abel, he also brought of the firstlings of his flock and of the fat thereof. And the LORD had respect unto Abel and to his offering: But unto Cain and to his offering he had not respect. And Cain was very wroth, and his countenance fell."* The Bible tells us that *"Cain was very wroth, and his countenance fell."* We see that because of the circumstance, this triggered negative emotions in the mind of Cain, including anger *(wroth)* and depression *(countenance fell)*. Cain allowed this triggering event to lead to a thought that preoccupied his mind, which, in turn, negatively affected his heart. God, knowing the heart of Cain, tried to intervene in Genesis 4:6 by asking Cain a series of questions in the attempt to have him acknowledge the process that was going on in his mind. *"And the LORD said unto Cain, Why art thou wroth? and why is thy countenance fallen?"* The Bible does not really record a response from Cain, so we think that we are safe to assume that he did not take God seriously. In not taking God seriously, the trigger that had become a thought now had become a full-forced craving. We find he acted upon this craving in a very destructive manner, not only for himself but for his brother, Abel. As we continue reading in Genesis, chapter 4, we see in verse 8 that Cain rose up against Abel and murdered him. *"And Cain talked with Abel his brother: and it came to pass, when they were in the field, that Cain rose up against Abel his brother, and slew him."* As we noted earlier in this book that in the life of Achan, Achan saw, coveted, took, hid and finally got caught. The same spiral downward happened in the life of Cain. In subsequent verses *(Genesis 4:9-15)*, we find God confronting Cain with his destructive behavior and the ultimate consequence of that destructive behavior. Addictive behavior is costly. Reformers Unanimous constantly reminds the student that there is a high cost for their destructive behavior. Unfortunately this high cost is shared amongst the family and friends of the individual.

My friends, we must be aware of negative thoughts and emotions. They can be a serious trigger!

2. PEOPLE AND PLACES

Seeing an old friend that you used to do drugs with or participate in destructive behavior with will bring up memories of that substance abuse (destructive behavior) and can become a trigger that will then lead into a craving and finally a repeat of that destructive action. Even driving passed a bar can be very difficult for someone who was addicted to alcohol, even if that bar was not where they drank.

In the Bible we see **many illustrations of individuals** that were a trigger for someone to perform destructive behavior. We have already illustrated in detail the effect that Jonadab had on **Amnon** *(II Samuel 13)*. Now, let's focus on **Rehoboam**, the King of Israel and son of Solomon. Rehoboam had just inherited the kingship of the Nation of Israel when he was confronted with a situation. This situation required a decision. He sought for counsel among the elderly, godly men who gave him godly advice. Rehoboam forsook the godly counsel and allowed the counsel of a group of younger, ungodly men to trigger a thought that led to a craving of complete dominance and control over the people of Israel. That craving finally led to Rehoboam acting out on his craving, which led to destructive consequences for himself and the Nation of Israel as a whole *(I Kings 12 and II Chronicles 10)*.

Samson was another individual that people and places were a significant trigger in his life. In Judges 14:1 it says, *"And Samson went down to Timnath, and saw a woman in Timnath of the daughters of the Philistines."* Samson's meso-cortico-limbic dopamine system was keenly conditioned in regards to sensual, sexual activity. Going down to the wrong place was a trigger. For there in Timnath, Samson saw the wrong type of women, which were the daughters of the Philistines. This viewing of these sensual, sexual women triggered a thought in Samson's life that became a craving, and as the story unfolds, Samson acts on that craving with ultimate, destructive consequences. We find Samson repeating this destructive behavior once again in Judges 16:1 – *"Then went Samson to Gaza, and saw there an harlot, and went in unto her."* Once again, Samson repeats this destructive pattern. He goes to the wrong place – Gaza. When at the wrong place, he sees a sensual, sexual woman, which triggers a thought that leads to a craving that Samson eventually acts upon with resultant, devastating consequences. Then, a third time Samson follows the same destructive pattern in Judges 16:4 – *"And it came to pass afterward, that he loved a woman in the valley of Sorek, whose name was Delilah."* Finally, Samson goes to the wrong place again, Sorek, and sees a sensual, sexual woman that is a trigger for him that sets off a thought followed by a craving that he acts upon. This trigger, unfortunately, ends in his own self destruction – Judges 16:30 – *"And Samson said, Let me die with the Philistines. And he bowed himself with all his might; and the house fell upon the lords, and upon all the people that were therein. So the dead which he slew at his death were more than they which he slew in his life."*

Another issue is peer pressure. Our strong need to "fit in" can drive us to "give in" to the mighty power of peer pressure. The belief that "everyone is doing it" has a tremendous pull on what a person who isn't participating can convince himself he really wants and needs.

At Reformers Unanimous we help the student identify certain people and places that could be a trigger and advise the student to stay away if at all possible. My friends, we must be very careful where we go and the people we associate with. People and places can be a tremendous trigger that will bring on a thought followed by a craving, thus, leading to addictive behavior with ultimate destructive consequences!

3. PICTURES

Pictures, whether they be on film, video, DVD, billboards or the Internet can be one of the more devastating triggers. God does detail this type of trigger in the Book of Ezekiel when He tells the prophet to *"dig now in the wall"* (Ezekiel 8:8). He tells him to *"Go in, and behold the wicked abominations that they do here"* (Ezekiel 8:9). God is talking about what the individuals had stored in their minds as pictures. Obviously, we store images in our minds. For the ancients of Israel (verse 10), it describes the type of images that they had stored in their minds – *"So I went in and saw; and behold every form of **creeping things**, and **abominable beasts**, and all the **idols of the house of Israel**, pourtrayed upon the wall round about."* And, it continues to say that these images were portrayed all around the wall. This wall is the wall of their minds. When, in their private times, they could go and recall these images. You, too, can go and recall images that are a trigger to a thought, to a craving and to an action. He goes on to say in Ezekiel 8:12 that when these individuals go to see these images, it is in the dark. *"Then said he unto me, Son of man, hast thou seen what the ancients of the house of Israel **do in the*** *dark, every man in the chambers of his imagery? for they say, The LORD seeth us not; the LORD hath forsaken the earth."* They think that the Lord cannot see them in the dark, that God is not able to see what they have stored on the walls of their mind. This type of trigger deals more with the area of pornography and sexual addiction. Even though this type of addiction can go on for many years without outward complications or consequences, there are devastating and deadly consequences associated with this behavior. In Ezekiel 8:17-18 it says, *"Then he said unto me, Hast thou seen this, O son of man? Is it a light thing to the house of Judah that they commit the abominations which they commit here? for they have filled the land with violence, and have returned to provoke me to anger: and, lo, they put the branch to their nose. Therefore will I also deal in fury: mine eye shall not spare, neither will I have pity: and though they cry in mine ears with a loud voice, yet will I not hear them."* The prophet of God goes on and illuminates the inward and outward destruction that occurs from this addictive behavior.

Reformers Unanimous instructs the students to eliminate from their possession any visual reminder of their past addictive behavior or anything that could remotely trigger a thought. We believe that it is better to be safe than sorry.

4. THINGS OR ITEMS

We have dealt with this already in the life of Achan. We detailed earlier in this book what transpired with

Achan when he saw the forbidden "things" in the city of Jericho. He saw, he coveted, he took, he hid and then he got caught.

Other things that can act as a trigger are any types of drug paraphernalia: Pipes, drugs, bongs, needles. To a cocaine addict, seeing a spilt package of Sweet 'n Low can even be a trigger to use again. For a prescription drug abuser, the sight of the amber-colored bottles that prescription medicines come in, an unattended prescription pad on the physician's desk or a friend's bathroom medicine cabinet can all be significant triggers. Certain types of clothing that you may see in your closet or someone else wearing can be a trigger. This is why as you enter Reformers Unanimous, whether it be through one of the over 700 local chapters or via one of the Discipleship Home's, we assist you in cleaning out the clutter! It is amazing how little we actually need to live. All things with any triggering notion need to go. They not only need to go but Reformers Unanimous will help replace those things with items that will assist you in your recovery without relapse (ie; Bible, friends, etc.)

5. SOUNDS

There are certain sounds that can be a trigger. Music would probably be one of the major sounds that can trigger a mind to start thinking about using, thus creating a craving followed by addictive behavior. You cannot over estimate the power that sounds can have on the human body and brain. For example, even the sound of a beer can being opened can be a trigger. We have found that music is the greatest sound trigger that exists. At Reformers Unanimous we encourage the student to eliminate any music that could possibly be a trigger and replace it with music that facilitates their walk with God. The right music can actually trigger you toward good thoughts, thus good cravings and good activity. It is like the old saying, "Garbage in garbage out" or in the latter case, "good in good out."

6. SMELLS

Smells such as smoke or even body odors of individuals that you used to use with can be significant triggers. The stench smell of the drug house you used to go to can be another trigger. Perfumes or colognes that in the past have been associated with use can be a trigger. Tequila used in making a Margarita can also be a strong trigger in someone's life. We do not take any potential trigger lightly at Reformers Unanimous. Every potential trigger is dealt with according to the Word of God. This is one of the reasons why our students can have a recovery without relapse.

7. IDLENESS

Idleness is often a sought after commodity in our culture. Those that have found it have found a devastating effect on their life. David is a prime example of idleness. David *(II Samuel 11:1)* had idle time because he was supposed to be with his men in battle. *"And it came to pass, after the year was expired, at the time when kings go forth to battle, that David sent Joab, and his* servants with him, and all Israel; and they destroyed the children of Ammon, and besieged Rabbah. But **David tarried still at Jerusalem**." David was not fulfilling his responsibility. He was not engaged in the right activity. He stayed at home with little to do. This gave him idle time. During this idle time, he found himself where he should not have been at that certain time. II Samuel 11:2 says, "*And it came to pass in an eveningtide, that **David arose from off his bed, and walked upon the roof of the king's house**: and from the roof he saw a woman washing herself; and the woman was very beautiful to look upon.*" This trigger of idleness led him to see a woman washing herself, which caused a thought. This thought is seen in verse 3 – "*And David sent and enquired after the woman. And one said, **Is not this Bathsheba**, the daughter of Eliam, the wife of Uriah the Hittite?*" Then, in verse 4, we see the craving take place – "*And **David** sent messengers, and **took her;** and **she came in unto him**, and **he lay with her;** for she was purified from her uncleanness: and she returned unto her house.*" As we read in verse 4, the craving led to the action. As with any vicious cycle, it ends with devastating consequences. We see this in verse 5 – "*And **the woman conceived**, and sent and told David, and said, I am with child.*" In the remainder of the story, we read that this child ends up dying after it is delivered. David, of course, tried to cover up his wrongdoings. And, in doing so, his actions led to the death of Uriah, Bathsheba's husband. **NOTE:** Anytime we allow a trigger to produce a thought, a craving and finally destructive, addictive behavior, there are consequences involved!

Idleness is associated with negative destructive behavior, as is found in Ecclesiastes 10:18 – ***"By much slothfulness the building decayeth; and through idleness of the hands the house droppeth through."*** We read in the Bible that part of the reason Sodom was destroyed was because of idleness. Ezekiel 16:49 says, *"Behold, this was the iniquity of thy sister **Sodom**, pride, fulness of bread, and **abundance of idleness** was in her and in her daughters, neither did she strengthen the hand of the poor and needy."*

One of the many reasons our nation is falling today is because of the abundance of idleness. Idleness can be a significant trigger in one's life! At Reformers Unanimous we teach a balanced lifestyle that incorporates the body, soul, and spirit. There is time for rest and relaxation but always in a balanced manner and with the appropriate accountability. The daily program at the Discipleship Home's is a structured well organized plan that allows proper time for the physical, psychological and spiritual realms of life. Each part of the person's life has its proper time of nutrition and exercise (expenditure) with the foundational part resting on the spiritual walk. If the spiritual walk is weak then the psychological and physical part will follow. On the other hand just because the physical and psychological parts are strong does not mean that the spiritual will follow suit. This is why balance is sought after with the spiritual life at the core.

8. CERTAIN ACTIVITIES

One of my patients that I treated for addiction to prescription pain medications told me this story regarding one of his triggers. This individual was a professional man that played golf frequently during his addiction to Percocet. He eventually was caught using drugs on the job and sent to a program where I was his medical physician. He shared with me that once he had become clean for approximately four months, he went out golfing. He said that things went well for the first three holes. He was having a great time. But, at the tee box of the fourth hole, there was a drinking fountain where the golfers would stop and get a drink. In fact, he said after every third hole there was a drinking fountain for the golfers. When he saw that first drinking fountain on the tee of the fourth hole, it caused shivers in his body. For you see, every time he would have the opportunity on the golf course to pass a drinking fountain, he would always take some Percocet, not knowing how long it would take him to get to the next drinking fountain. He identified this as a trigger. He discussed this with me at length and obviously was able to overcome this trigger. It does not affect him anymore like it used to. This illustrates, however, that something as trivial as a drinking fountain on a golf course, something innocent in and of itself, something that is inanimate, can be a strong trigger!

9. LONELINESS

The Bible tells us in Genesis 2:18, *"And the LORD God said, It is not good that the man should be alone; I will make him an help meet for him.*" This verse is making reference to God making Adam a *"help meet" for life.* We believe, though, that there is also an underlining principle here that it is not good for us (man or woman) to be alone for any significant amount of time. Generally speaking, isolation is a dangerous place to be. One of the signs that someone is relapsing into their addictive, destructive behavior is isolation. If someone needs to be alone or if someone needs to spend time alone searching for God's will in their life, there must be accountability; there must be a safety net by the individual's authority so that this loneliness (isolation) will not trigger addictive behavior.

We see this (loneliness/isolation) illustrated in the life of Elijah when he had a great victory followed by a threatening statement by the queen, Jezebel. One of things Elijah did was isolate from his friend. We also see this illustrated in the life of Jonah. After a remarkable revival in Nineveh, Jonah became dissatisfied and depressed. We find him sitting outside the city all alone. Isolation or loneliness if not done properly can lead to a distorted way of thinking. This distorted thinking can lead us to entertain doing many things we would not normally do.

Loneliness (isolation) can be a very strong trigger in one's life!

10. HUNGER
This is illustrated in the life of Esau in the Book

of Genesis. In Genesis 25, we find Esau out in the field hunting. When he returned from his hunting expedition, he was so hungry that he was faint. Genesis 25:29 says, *"And Jacob sod pottage: and Esau came from the field, and he was faint:"* This hunger was a trigger which led Esau to a thought which, in turn, led him to a craving for food. He acted upon this craving at any cost! He comes to the point in verse 30 where he dramatizes his circumstance and makes the statement, **"Feed me**, *I pray thee, with that same red pottage;* **for I am faint**: *therefore was his name called Edom."* He acted as if he was going to die if he did not receive any food at that moment in time. Jacob goes on to give him the pottage but at the price of Esau's birthright. As you study the life of Esau, you find that he would later on regret this activity that he partook in. As with Esau, many addicts regret activities that they have done in the past. This again illustrates the need for a balanced life with the body, soul and spirit.

Reformers Unanimous encourages a healthy diet with regularly scheduled meals and snacks.

11. FATIGUE

When we have an overwhelming sense of fatigue, we will start to feel as if we deserve some form of reward for our fatigue, which can then trigger a thought followed by a craving and summed up by an action. When everything is said and done, our fatigue made us think that we deserved something pleasurable! Reformers Unanimous recommends a healthy pattern of sleep for each of its students. Regularly scheduled times to go to bed, with a healthy "go to bed routine" and arising from sleep at a planned time are a part of the daily program.

12. TOUCH

A certain touch by another individual or by us touching an inanimate object that was a part of our addictive behavior can also be a trigger. This can be closely associated with the trigger of things that we discussed earlier.

13. TASTE

Certain tastes can be conditioned with certain activities. These tastes can be triggers to previous addictive, destructive behavior. Again nothing is taken lightly.

14. SOCIAL CUES

Social cues are powerful and usually not identified as a trigger. We eat because someone brought a cake to work or because we are bored. We crave certain foods not based on what our body is telling us it needs for nourishment, but because it is a specific holiday or social event. Responding to our appetites, in general, is triggered more by social habit than anything else. I travel on airplanes a lot and caught myself drinking diet soda's "just because I could and it was offered." This appetite grew out of control until the only thing I was drinking was carbonated soda. I did not see it as a trigger until I made a choice to change my habit. It was not until I sensed the specific and strong urge return while on my next flight and I was confronted with a diet soda. Social cues can be powerful triggers.

15. PAST ABUSE OR NEGLECT

Remembrance of past abuse or neglect can be a devastating trigger. Addictive behavior can be triggered by childhood trauma or a sense of rejection that was instilled into a child's thought process. Children's needs and desires start out innocent. But, when abuse, neglect or other serious family dysfunction is present in a child's life, their inward appetites may become twisted and harmful to themselves and others around them. The extended deprivation of basic needs or the presence of intense and extensive negative attention causes children to experience a sense of emptiness that runs deeper than many of us can ever know. A child will then seek fulfillment many times in harmful ways. I have talked to many students who have come through our program with sexual addictions. Many admitted to me that exposure to sexually graphic material and real life instances started their sexual addictions. Remembering these past events and meditating upon them can be a strong trigger for them to return to their addictive behaviors.

16. PARENTAL INFLUENCES AND LEARNING

I have often stated that during my learning development I studied people and their behavior more than I realized. Hero's, parents, siblings, caregivers and teachers all affect our learned patterns and behaviors. These can become triggers to destructive behavior in future years. When we watch a stressed parent turn to the television, refrigerator, workout room, beer can, other women, cigarettes, Vicoden, Zanax and the like, we believe that these are effective ways of making us feel better when we are stressed also. We also witness adults using food, alcohol, drugs or relationships as means of rewarding themselves for some accomplishment or other activity. Either way, we are learning from their examples that such behaviors can bring instant feelings of pleasure and relief from whatever stressful, painful situation we are in. We view these habits as "fixer uppers" to problems. Generally these built-in or learned triggers will not surface until challenged with the truth. At Reformers Unanimous we like to explore these learned triggers so that the individual can acknowledge them and then deal with them according to the truth.

17. WRONG VIEW OF SELF IMAGE

The world is focused on helping people develop a "better self esteem." Many programs use this avenue as their primary premise. People who are struggling with low self esteem and a low sense of self worth are held prisoner by a set of irrational and false beliefs as to who they really are. The reasons for their distorted self image are many, such as physical characteristics, rejection, loss of loved ones without closure, etc. These are just a few of the experiences I have tried to help individuals with. Often, deep wounds that have never had the opportunity to heal properly is another trigger that has to be dealt with on an ongoing basis. Fake beliefs can also drive people into an ever-increasing spiral of negative thoughts that may become a set of self-fulfilling prophecies. These strongly-held beliefs can push their destructive behavior out of control and actually confirm (at least in their own mind) that what they believe is true. When we accept a set of false beliefs, they will become the driving force behind our choices, our appetites and our lives. Before our behavior can begin to change, we will have to face the reality of the beliefs we have been holding and come to an understanding of who we really are in Christ. The Reformers Unanimous curriculum helps the individual realize who they are in Jesus Christ, and the rich, Godly heritage awaiting them. Reformers Unanimous helps the individual have a Biblically-based self image, which propels them to Godly living.

So, in light of all of the above potential trigger mechanisms, and again, this is NOT an exhaustive list, we must be careful what we allow to come into our lives. This is imperative for a recovery without relapse. By the power of God, through His indwelling Holy Spirit it is available to all those that will follow. Remember failure only occurs when we fail to follow the Truth.

A trigger can be the beginning of an individual's worst nightmare. Just like the first few grains of snow that start down a hillside and trigger an avalanche, a relapse can also be triggered by what seems like the smallest of events or emotions. Knowing those triggers and making a plan of escape, based on the Truth, before you hit the steep slope is a key to your recovery without a relapse.

God wants us to become aware of our thoughts and emotions and turn to Him to obtain grace and power for control over the triggers instead of them controlling us. As we do this, cravings and their associated, addictive, destructive behavior is reduced and in fact can be eliminated. We, thus, become less fearful and more confident that we can, through the grace of God, life a victorious life without resorting to addictive, destructive behavior.

Since a trigger is the very start of the addiction cycle, it has the least power and momentum. This is the place where the addiction loop is most easily stopped. In order for our strategy to work, it must meet certain criteria. The criteria are as follows:

1. It must be founded on the Truth.

2. It must be immediately available to the individual.

3. It must be something possible to do in the real world.

4. It must be something that will be successful when done properly.

5. It must be something that the individual is capable of doing.

6. It must be able to work for all triggers.

If the above criteria are met (which they are) and the individual is desirous to obtain victory over the trigger (that's up to you), then the addiction cycle can be stopped.

God has outlined a plan in the Bible that, if followed properly, will give us the victory. So, what is God's plan? God's plan is a multifaceted exit strategy. The most effective exit strategy is based on the following five parts:

1. THOUGHT CAPTIVATION

This is the foundational principle of the exit strategy and is based on the meditation of God's Word. As we recognize a trigger and the thought generated by it, we must choose to mediate on God's Word. We must cast down the triggering thought and bring into captivity the thought associated with meditating on God's Word. This is exampled for us in II Corinthians 10:5 – *"Casting down imaginations, and every high thing that exalteth itself against the knowledge of God, and bringing into captivity every thought to the obedience of Christ;"* Any thought generated by a trigger is going to be a dangerous, damaging thought to our relationship with Jesus Christ, to our walk in the Truth. These thoughts must be "cast down" and done away with before they cause great harm. We have a tendency to meditate on these negative thoughts. We need to cast them down or in other words "get rid of them." We are to refuse to think of them, refuse to dwell on them. God teaches us in II Corinthians 10:5 to cast those thoughts down and captivate godly thoughts. We are to captivate those thoughts that stabilize and strengthen our walk with Him. A craving generally starts off small and then gains momentum. At the earliest evidence of a thought or craving, we are to cast it down – GET RID OF IT BY MEDITATING ON GOD'S WORD! We must not allow the craving to gain any momentum or strength. On the contrary, may we allow God's Word to gain momentum and strength in our life. The best way to allow God's Word to gain momentum in your life is to meditate on the seven things He tells us to do, everyday, in the Bible. Many become paralyzed by procrastination when they are facing a trigger. We must ask ourselves when faced with a trigger, "What can I do right now toward defeating this trigger?" We need to concentrate on doing the following seven things. In meditating on these seven things and then doing these seven things everyday of our life it will leave little room for any destructive, addictive behavior to resurface again in our life. These seven things are:

A. Daily search the Scriptures.

- Read, study and memorize the Bible.
- Acts 17:11 – *"These were more noble than those in Thessalonica, in that they received the word with all readiness of mind, and searched the scriptures daily, whether those things were so."*

B. Daily take up your cross.

- Look to help others.
- Luke 9:23 – "*And he said to them all, If any man will come after me, let him deny himself, and take up his cross daily, and follow me.*"

C. Daily exhort.

- Look to encourage others.
- Hebrews 3:13 – "*But exhort one another daily, while it is called To day; lest any of you be hardened through the deceitfulness of sin.*"

D. Daily die.

- Ask God for His will and way to be done and not ours.
- I Corinthians 15:31 – "*I protest by your rejoicing which I have in Christ Jesus our Lord, I die daily.*"

E. Daily perform your vows.

- Make sure you are doing what you promised God you would do.
- Psalm 61:8 – "*So will I sing praise unto thy name for ever, that I may daily perform my vows.*"

F. Daily praise God.

- Meditate on how great God is.
- Psalm 119:164 – "*Seven times a day do I praise thee because of thy righteous judgments.*"

G. Daily pray.

- Spend time throughout the day communicating with God.
- Psalm 86:3 – "*Be merciful unto me, O Lord: for I cry unto thee daily.*"

When faced with a trigger make up your mind to keep walking with God by meditating on and doing the seven things God commands us to do in His Word. This will be foundational in your recovery without relapse.

Here are some other verses from the Bible that you can put to memory so that you can bring them to mind at a latter date to meditate on them when a trigger confronts you.

II Corinthians 10:5 - "*Casting down imaginations, and every high thing that exalteth itself against the knowledge of God, and bringing into captivity every thought to the obedience of Christ;*"

Proverbs 3:5-6 – "*Trust in the LORD with all thine heart; and lean not unto thine own understanding. In all thy ways acknowledge him, and he shall direct thy paths.*"

2. AVOIDANCE OR ESCAPE

With any triggering event, God always promises a way of escape. I Corinthians 10:13 says, "*There hath no temptation taken you but such as is common to man:*"

but God is faithful, who will not suffer you to be tempted above that ye are able; but will with the temptation also make a way to escape, that ye may be able to bear it." The easiest way to deal with a trigger is to avoid them at all cost. Proverbs 1:10 says, "My son, if sinners entice thee, consent thou not." Just stay away. Sometimes it is as simple as that. You must cut off all contact with people that are drug users or are associated with it. Avoiding a certain place or leaving a certain place when a trigger surfaces is a safe way to protect yourself. People who truly love and care for you and your recovery will understand if you have to leave an event because you are being confronted with a trigger. Be honest with them! They will help watch out for you in the future. The Bible says in Proverbs 1:15 – "My son, walk not thou in the way with them; refrain thy foot from their path:" Also, Proverbs 4:14-15 – "Enter not into the path of the wicked, and go not in the way of evil men. Avoid it, pass not by it, turn from it, and pass away." To the best of your ability, avoid all known triggers.

3. REMEMBERING

Remember what your addictive behavior cost you and your loved ones in the past and where this trigger will lead you again. Make a crash card (illustration below) of the negative consequences of your past addictive behavior.

1. Almost died.

2. Remember withdrawals.

3. Family almost lost.

4. Financial disaster.

5. Family and friends disappointed.

6. Testimony destroyed.

We tend to forget how bad our lives had become and the great difficulties we put our families through. Complacency can cost you your family, finances, and even your life. The Bible has numerous examples of the high cost inflicted on the individual and their families by their addictive/destructive behavior. Cain ends up murdering his brother and having his life cursed by God. Samson caused much heart-ache to his parents and then ends up dying in the midst of his enemies. Achan's destructive behavior caused the death of his entire family including himself not to mention the Israelite soldiers that died in the battle against Ai. If you fail to follow and end up relapsing the devastation will be out there waiting for you as it was in the past. There are no exceptions to this rule. Remember, you and your loved ones will pay again.

4. ACCOUNTABILITY PARTNER

Here at Reformers Unanimous we believe that every student should have an accountability partner. Someone they can turn to at a moments notice to seek their advice and counsel. Someone who has the liberty to check-up on them with complete honesty in return.

If you feel you cannot confront your trigger alone, contact your accountability partner. Your accountability partner can be your pastor, RU director, RU leader, spiritual mentor, or even a godly family member or friend. This person must be someone you can trust who takes your trigger and recovery seriously but graciously. You need someone who will guide you into the truth of God's Word. Don't wait too long! Do whatever is necessary to get out of the situation that compromises your walk with God.

5. LIVE IN THE MOMENT

When we find ourselves fantasizing of what things could be like or what we would like things to be like, we need to jerk ourselves back into the reality of the moment, the reality of today and be content where we are right now. Contentment will extinguish many fiery triggers. The Bible puts a premium on contentment. The following are some verses that need to be mediated on in the appropriate setting:

Philippians 4:11 – *"Not that I speak in respect of want: for I have learned, in whatsoever state I am, therewith to be content."*

I Timothy 6:8 – *"And having food and raiment let us be therewith content."*

Hebrews 13:5 – *"Let your conversation be without covetousness; and be content with such things as ye have: for he hath said, I will never leave thee, nor forsake thee."*

Lack of contentment in our lives will result in destructive behavior. In the Book of III John, we read of a man named Diotrephes. Diotrephes was an individual that was discontent with his life. His discontentment brought great harm to himself and his local church. Discontentment will result in destructive behavior in your own life with resultant devastation to your loved ones.

Chapter 5
An Ending Appeal

*A*LL OF US IN LIFE END UP WITH A personal belief system. We all have one. Although you may have never sat down and defined what your belief system is, it is fully operative and working in your life at all times. It deals with what you believe about the world in which you live, about the people and about how events and circumstances affect you. Whatever your personal belief system is, it determines how you respond to events that come into your life. What is needed in all of us is a personal belief system that is based solely on the Word of God. In more basic terms, our basic belief system IS the Word of God. For what we have come to find out through the Reformers Unanimous curriculum is that Truth makes free. The Truth is Jesus Christ; the Truth is the Word of God – the Bible. So, to walk in freedom, our personal belief system MUST be the Truth. When your personal belief system is the Truth, you will be relaxed and confident because you know that God is in control of your journey. This is how life is when your personal belief system is based on the Truth. Having your personal belief system based on the Truth will completely change your life. However, if your belief system is based on an assumption or a lie, it will have equally devastating effects. Such as, if you believe that using alcohol, addictive drugs or destructive behaviors will better your life, it just isn't so. And, we only injure ourselves further by continuing to believe on it and walk in it. So, you will fail to achieve freedom from dependency if you go about life with a belief system based on a lie.

A personal belief system based on the Truth – **THE WORD OF GOD** – will sustain you through every occurrence that life brings to you. It will make even your best days brighter and save you countless hours of misery and needless suffering. It will help you see that events you may have lamented for weeks, months or even years will turn out to be the best events that ever happened to you as noted in Romans 8:28 – *"And we know that all things work together for good to them that love God, to them who are the called according to his purpose."*

Here at Reformers Unanimous we have learned and we teach how essential it is to live according to the empowering presence of the Holy Spirit of God in our lives. He is the only One that will see us through the difficult times of despair, hardship, grief and despondency that seem to regularly occur to us all. The Holy Spirit brings a smile to our face that is more than just a brave veneer in the face of adversity. Reformers Unanimous teaches, in its curriculum, that through the indwelling, empowerment of the Holy Spirit of God in our lives, God directs and will sustain us in everything that we think, say and do. He gives us hope for the future. It is liberating to be free from the events that knock on our door.

Have you had something happen to you that seemed really bad at the time but later on turned out to be beneficial? Everyone we have asked that question to here at Reformers Unanimous has been able to remember several events like that. It is time to look at all the events in the light of the glorious Gospel of Jesus Christ and His blessed Word. God wants everything in your life to benefit you so that through you He can build His kingdom. Although events may hurt you, take something from you or bring you pain, they are there for your growth and understanding as well as your total and complete benefit as His dear child.

We have made the statement that a trigger leads to a thought that leads to a craving that leads to addictive, destructive behavior. Addictive, destructive behavior often feels like it strikes without warning. But, with a Spirit-led soul, we can develop a sensitivity to the internal and external triggers that stimulate our addictive, destructive behavior.

Daily, we should take a moment to bring awareness to how our emotions, distorted thought processes, and automatic interpretation of events can feed into triggers, then into a thought, followed by the craving with ultimate destructive, addictive behavior.

In reality, all addictions and destructive behaviors are a search for relief and answers. But, the answers are never to be found out there. The answer is the following: JESUS IN YOU AND YOU IN JESUS. This is what is waiting to be discovered here at Reformers Unanimous. What you have been doing with drugs, alcohol or destructive behaviors have only been suppressing the Holy Spirit's ability and power to overcome the difficulties that surround your life. Please, join us at Reformers Unanimous and learn how to heal the problems underlying your dependency rather than being a victim of them. In the process, learn how to live a victorious life in Jesus Christ. What remains and what is more difficult to heal are the problems that drove you to alcohol and drugs in the first place. They are the weak links in your chain. Unless you allow God to heal the underlying conditions that have created and maintained your dependency, those problems will lead you back to the alcohol, drugs and destructive behaviors over and over and over again. Please! May we introduce you to the Truth? May we introduce you to Jesus Christ? My friend, He will finally make you free.

For the sake of those you love, for the sake of God's good Name, and for the sake of your own relationship with your Savior, deal with your triggers and do it immediately. You will always find God ready and willing to assist you! *Jeremiah 33:3 – "Call unto me, and I will answer thee, and show thee great and mighty things, which thou knowest not."*

Appendix A
MATT'S TESTIMONY

THROUGHOUT MY LIFE, THE RELATIONSHIP I HAD WITH JESUS CHRIST was very unstable, very double-minded. I felt that my walk with the Lord could never truly grow due to the unending cycle of habitual sin that left me crippled and unable to be effective as a Christian witness. I would get sick of how often I would disobey the Lord by feeding my lustful addiction. My fellowship with the Lord would be broken for weeks and even months at a time due to the heavy condemnation I was feeling. I would get so defeated by the lies of Satan, which would result in me ignoring God for awhile until He would chasten and break me, bringing me back to repentance. I found myself tied up in my own shame, trying to win the battle all on my own. I would try to do it in my own power with God as an afterthought. I did not have the kind of relationship Jesus wanted me to have where He was my complete strength.

As I was about to be married (in my late twenties), I was determined to find victory from my addiction to pornography. I sought accountability from friends at my church. I put up web blockers on my computer, joined sexual-addicts anonymous as well as some Christian faith-based addiction programs. None of them gave me true, lasting victory. One of the first expectations that collapsed on me was the hope that my pornography addiction would cease to be an issue after I got married. It not only was still a struggle, it caused me fear to tell my wife the truth that I was continuing to fall. I, however, finally had the courage to tell her. It justifiably damaged her trust in me. During that time, God began to change my heart and mind about a lot of things that I had previously believed. God began to make me recognize how truly compromising I was riding the fence between being a follower of Christ and a follower of the world.

My wife finally divorced me. I found the divorce very difficult to deal with. Satan used feelings of rejection to further bring me into my bondage. I also got laid off at my job because of the declining economy. The Lord was very merciful during this time, and He began to point me to the right church He knew I needed to be attending. It was awesome to see the Lord start to work in ways I needed maturing in. It was while attending this church that I saw for the first time Reformers Unanimous. The Reformers Unanimous Program was held every Friday night at this church. Its structure, principles and challenges were so Biblically based that

I knew that it was going to be far more successful in my life than all the other programs I was involved in. Although I started getting involved in Reformers Unanimous, I did not take it seriously as I should have nor was I getting involved with the daily journal. Being unemployed for three months while still feeling the pain of my divorce brought me back into slothfulness with movies, television, video games and pornography talking a hold on my life. I stopped going to church and just wanted to give up.

My pastor reached out to me and suggested that I, once again, be faithful to the Reformers Unanimous Program as well as the church services. Immediately when I heard his advice, I knew it was the right thing to do. I knew God would have me in church and participating faithfully in the Reformers Unanimous meetings on Friday nights and actively engaging in the curriculum and daily journal. For, you see, down deep I wanted to grow and have a relationship with the Lord Jesus Christ that was pure, consistent, surrendered and full of joy.

That week I started again with the RU meeting, the daily journal and attending the church services. I started to be faithful and began to develop deep, Spiritual friendships. God caused an explosion in my walk with Him. As I met with Him early in the morning in diligent study and prayer, He blessed me in ways I did not expect. For the first time in my life I was an encouragement to others around me. God started to develop Spiritual leadership qualities I never had before. I was always a follower, and for the first time, I was the encourager. I was investing in the lives of other men and women and bearing their burdens. I started to mature and be that servant leader God always wanted me to be. What was even more profound was the Biblical insights taught by Brother Curington were applied when I would let God take control and live in me.

Without much effort and only a willing spirit, I experienced amazing, divine appointments. I would run into individuals with specific burdens, needs or questions. Without even expecting it, God would take the things I learned and speak through me with words I could not even communicate on my own. And, it would meet the needs of that individual at the exact time they needed it. It has gotten me so excited to see God work in such a way that it has matured my faith.

Through the Reformers Unanimous Program, I have recognized some very important truths that are key to having victory from my lustful addiction. First, I found as I met with God consistently every morning and throughout the day, my Spiritual armor that I put on became increasingly thicker and stronger day by day as I would consistently cast down lustful thoughts Satan would throw at me. As the days would go by, where I would remain pure and dwell on those thoughts, it would be harder for the devil to infiltrate that armor. However, when I gave into those thoughts and started to dwell on them and consume my mind, that armor would completely crumble. I would have to spend the time in repentance to the Lord and meet with Him to allow Him to hold me and build back my Spiritual armor. Otherwise, my lustful addiction would continue to grow.

Secondly, I recognized that I had held onto the triggers that constantly led me back to my strongholds. I never really surrendered those triggers to God until I came to Reformers Unanimous. I began to recognize that they were strongholds that I had never broken free of. The biggest trigger was my addiction to movies, television and entertainment. Being talented in video production all of my life, Hollywood was fully integrated in me. I loved it, and it was the hardest thing to give up. Not only did entertainment waste my time when I could have been devoting myself to Godly, eternally-minded things, but it is impossible to escape the very hint of sexual imagery that is abundant in practically everything we watch. Even in the most innocent of shows there is still sexual imagery. Getting it out of my life has done wonders in my sexual purity. I had to even make a commitment to cut out the web surfing that I did religiously. Another trigger (stronghold) that I realized was my eating habits. Even if I committed to staying pure from my entertainment addiction, the moment I decided to go to unhealthy foods, it would start to slow my metabolism, making me tired and sluggish and causing me to lose focus on what I was doing. This, of course, would start my desire to sit back, relax and have entertainment back into my life. Unhealthy foods have been a strong addiction to break free from. But, when I strongly committed myself to the Lord in this area, I have seen a major roadblock come between Satan and me. Thus, it has been difficult for Satan to get through and attack me with the arrows that would so easily pierce me. Jesus preached the Sermon on the Mount in Matthew 5:29-30 – *"And if thy right eye offend thee, pluck it out, and cast it from thee: for it is profitable for thee that one of thy members should perish, and not that thy whole body should be cast into hell. And if thy right hand offend thee, cut it off, and cast it from thee: for it is profitable for thee that one of thy members should perish, and not that thy whole body should be cast into hell."* I had to literally pluck out all sight from entertainment. Otherwise, it would continue to draw me in. I also had to cut off all consumption of unhealthy food. Otherwise, my armor would break down and Satan could find a way back into my life.

The third thing that I recognized at being key to giving me true victory is my continued, daily, Christ-empowered love to encourage fellow believers to be generous and kind and reach out to others with compassion and Godly love. In Hebrews 3:13 it says, *"But exhort one another daily, while it is called To day; lest any of you be hardened through the deceitfulness of sin."* When I am led and guided by God to do His will to encourage and exhort others, it gives me such a joy and peace knowing that I am doing the Lord's work. As I daily do this, it keeps me focused on what God wants me to do.

The fourth thing I see in my own life, especially lately, is that I am asking God to get me to a place where I can be transformed the most. To use whatever means possible for Him to change me is one of the hardest things to pray for. Because I know that adversity, trials and pain are the hardest things to go through. I know God usually has that in mind when I asked for transformation, because it is what will cause the most growth. The only factor that is needed with this is my total willingness and endurance to get through His trials, or, otherwise, I will normally do what I have done my whole life and that is to cling onto my pornographic addiction to get through the pain. Immediately when pain and distress come into my life, I have to cling tightly to the Lord, spending as much of my free time as I possibly can alone with Him each day. I cry out to Him through my pain and developing a devoted walk with Him has only brought incredible Spiritual rewards in my life and has increased my genuine love for God and others. The moment I stop clinging to the Lord, I expose myself to Satan who will constantly pound on the areas I am the weakest. Spending time with the Lord with humility in the morning and praying and meditating throughout the day is the first and most important part of having true victory. If I don't cut off all the triggers that Satan uses, my consistent walk with the Lord will fail. If I don't' exhort and encourage consistently, day by day, I will become more focused on myself, and it will lead me back to my fleshly desires.

Lastly, I have to be open and willing for the Lord to use circumstances in my life to transform me. I have to be ready to hold onto the Lord tightly when that adversity starts to flood into my life. Taking a hold of the Lord and not allowing the trials of life to sweep me away only strengthens me in ways that I have never seen before. I have to remember that if I am passive and start to be uncommitted and ignorant to these truths, I immediately have to recommit these things to the Lord. When I fall and give into my lustful temptations, I know I have to immediately repent and recommit so that Satan does not bring me into shame and discouragement.

Thank the Lord for His abundant mercy, and His promise to those who walk after the Spirit. Romans 8:1 says, *"There is therefore now no condemnation to them which are in Christ Jesus, who walk not after the flesh, but after the Spirit."*

Appendix B

Enter Not Into Temptation
Benjamin Burks

"*THEN SAITH JESUS UNTO THEM, All ye shall be offended because of me this night: for it is written, I will smite the shepherd, and the sheep of the flock shall be scattered abroad. But after I am risen again, I will go before you into Galilee. Peter answered and said unto him, Though all [men] shall be offended because of thee, [yet] will I never be offended. Jesus said unto him, Verily I say unto thee, That this night, before the cock crow, thou shalt deny me thrice. Peter said unto him, Though I should die with thee, yet will I not deny thee. Likewise also said all the disciples. Then cometh Jesus with them unto a place called Gethsemane, and saith unto the disciples, Sit ye here, while I go and pray yonder. And he took with him Peter and the two sons of Zebedee, and began to be sorrowful and very heavy. Then saith he unto them, My soul is exceeding sorrowful, even unto death: tarry ye here, and watch with me. And he went a little further, and fell on his face, and prayed, saying, O my Father, if it be possible, let this cup pass from me: nevertheless not as I will, but as thou [wilt]. And he cometh unto the disciples, and findeth them asleep, and saith unto Peter, What, could ye not watch with me one hour? Watch and pray, that ye enter not into temptation: the spirit indeed [is] willing, but the flesh [is] weak." Matthew 26:31-41*

There are twenty-five million addicts in America today and each addict directly affects the lives of four other people. This makes up 100 million people in America today who are looking for hope and answers, and they don't know that the answer is found in the local church. They don't know that God called and ordained the local New Testament church to deal with these Spiritual problems, and they are indeed Spiritual problems, not a disease. If they are a disease, it's the only one you have to get a license in order to spread. If it's a disease, it's the only one they advertise for billions of dollars per year saying, "Come get some so you can die." If it's a disease, it's the only one that people give as a Christmas present. It is not a disease; it is sin. What can wash away my sin? Nothing but the blood of Jesus. What can make me whole again? Oh, precious is the flow. There's a fountain filled with blood drawn from Immanuel's veins, and sinners plunged beneath that flood lose all their guilty stain. Amen! I appreciate that song about the cross, because I think that's a place a Christian ought to go to daily to experience the resurrection power.

To begin, the Reformers Unanimous Ministry started

in 1996. Previous to that there was a man that grew up in a good church, grew up in a Christian school and was going to go to Bible College. He was enrolled and completed everything that needed to be done prior to his first class but decided to take a year off and, unfortunately, found some bad friends to hang around with. That one year turned into ten years of drugs and alcohol. This man's name is Steven Curington. He hurt everybody that ever loved him, his mom and dad, brothers, friends, and family. He grew his hair out real long, down to his waist. Cocaine was his choice drug along with alcohol He loved the party scene atmosphere. He couldn't hold a job, and he was in and out of jail and in and out of struggles the entire ten years. Let me just say, in that ten years, no one from church came to see him to try to help him. To be quite honest, they really did not know *how* to help him. His mom even worked in the Christian school and was on staff and still not one person from the church came by to say, "Steve, whenever you are ready we've got the answers; just let us know." By the way, I don't think that it is much different across America, because the devil has fooled us into thinking, "Well, their problem is a little bit deeper and a little bit bigger than what we can deal with." The problem is sin, and we don't deal with sin, Christ does. All we have to do is be a bridge to get them to Him.

At the end of the ten years, Steve had an accident in a neighborhood where nobody lived. In fact, it was all brand new construction. He put his money together with a friend of his, and they went there to get some drugs. He started to pull out of the newly-constructed neighborhood where nobody lived except for one person right on the corner of a three-way stop. Steve went to pull out of the three-way stop, and he was t-boned by a drunk driver. He had hit the gas instead of the break, went through the brick wall of a home being built, came out the other side and was finally thrown from his vehicle into the ditch of the only home that someone occupied. The lady heard the crash, called 911 and went outside to compress Steve's bleeding wounds. She said the sounds of death were so bad that she had to go back inside. The ambulance soon arrived and took Steve to the hospital. Shortly after, he recovered from the accident. However, while he was in the hospital, his Sunday School teacher from ten years before came to visit him. He gave him a Bible and told him, "Steve, we don't know how to help you, but the answer's in this Book." Steve began to read the Bible his Sunday school teacher had brought him, and he came across the verse that said, "And ye shall know the truth, and the truth shall make you free." That verse rang true in his mind, because in secular programs he heard for ten years, "Only the truth sets free." But, according to the secular world, truth can be anything. They say truth is information. They say information is power, but it's not. Knowing Him is power. They say truth can be an ashtray, a doorknob or anything else you deem as truth. But, we know the Bible says that Jesus is Truth. In the days following his accident, Steve began to meditate on the one truth and that is *"only*

Jesus can make me free." He knew he was saved, but he also knew that he wasn't free. Did you know that saved people can backslide? By the way, we would have revival if God's people would stop looking at other people trying to figure out if they're saved or not. If you don't think they're saved, go witness to them and try to win them to Christ. Instead of wasting all of your oxygen, save your breath and use it for the glory of God.

Steve began to meditate on the truth outlined in God's Word, and as soon as he got out of the hospital and recovered, he went back to the church. As he sat there with his long hair and blue jeans in the last row on the left-hand side of the church, people came by and said, enthusiastically, "Welcome home, Steve!" By the way, isn't that what a church is supposed to do? The church is not a museum or a social club. The church is supposed to be a Spiritual hospital where sick people, spiritually speaking, can come and get help! Where else are they going to go for an answer if they are spiritually sick and need help? Steve came into the church and began to grow and develop underneath the pastor. He began to get more and more involved in church functions. As an added note, I love the story of Steve and the all-night teen activity. They went out and played some games as well as watched some movies until 4:30 or 5:00 in the morning. On his way home, he passed by his old friends. He saw their car weaving down the road, and he saw the pain on all of their faces. He started to cry and realized it had been six months since he had used drugs, and he realized that he had been made free.

Soon, Steve started a Bible study for addicts on Friday nights in the smallest room of the church. He started his Bible study on Friday night because he realized addicts won't come on Sunday morning. By experience, he knew they had already been in their addiction for 48 hours so why would they want to come to church! They aren't even awake yet! He said, "Preacher, I'm going to start a Bible study on Friday night, and if we can get them here on Friday night and get them in the curriculum, then that'll lead them to the real support group which is the local church because that's what they need!" Steve knew that they needed to learn to walk with God, because the man or woman who walks with God will always arrive at the right destination. Brother Curington began to grow and develop even more after he started his Friday night addiction program at the church. Sometimes he had only 8, 10, 12 or 15 people at the most. One week the attendance would be 15, and the next week it would be down to 10. Steve never gave up! Now, we have over 275 people in our auditorium on Friday nights in the addiction program. You talk about a live crowd! We have a great time. We have all walks of life attending the Friday night program: ex-prostitutes, drug addicts and alcoholics. Their family members come with them, and they, along with the addict, learn how to live the crucified Christian life. It's not just happening in Rockford. It's happening all across America.

As Steve began to grow more and more in the truths of God's Word and continued developing the Reformers Unanimous Program he started, he met a young lady in the church. They quickly fell in love and decided to get married. He went over to her house one Sunday night after church to talk to her mother about asking her hand in marriage. As he sat there in front of her mom (nervous, of course) he told them the story about his former life of drugs and alcohol and how he renewed his life with Jesus Christ. He then started talking about the accident he had that started the wheels spinning toward his complete recovery from drugs, alcohol and the like. When he finished his story, Lori's mom got up from the table and left, visibly shaken. He thought, "Man, this is a bad way to get started with your future mother-in-law." She was gone for a while, but when she came back, she had a clipping from the Rockford Register Star, our local newspaper. She opened it up and said, "Steve, does that look familiar to you?" He said "Yes, that's the car in the ditch, the day after my accident three or four years ago. Why do you have that?" She said, "Because I was the one that lived in that house and called 911 and saved your life." That's his mother-in-law today! God had a plan for Steve's life, and he used his future mother-in-law to accomplish it. WOW! God is good.

Reformers Unanimous is a wonderful ministry and an exciting program. What the addicted person needs is someone who will say, "Follow me as I follow Christ." We must be a living example to them. We must work through the curriculum with them. We can never change the way a person acts until we can change the way a person thinks. Our meditators get all messed up when we think on bad and negative things. What are you thinking about? *"For as he thinketh in his heart, so is he:" (Proverbs 23:7)* We have to deal with our own stubborn habits before we can help other people with their stubborn habits. Joy can never be found in a bottle. Joy is a fruit of the Holy Spirit of God, and you cannot be filled with a substance and with God at the same time. Ephesians 5:18 says, "And be not drunk with wine, wherein is excess; but be filled with the Spirit;" We all know how wine controls us. So, don't give yourself to wine. Let the Spirit control you.

There is a pattern that I want to expound on; a pattern that I've noticed in churchgoers as well as non-churchgoers. This pattern is a vicious cycle, and it all starts with a wound. We all have wounds that come into our lives. These are difficulties, injustices and hurts. Sometimes these are things that we vote for; the wages of our sin. You could say that we bring it on ourselves. When we do wrong, it does hurt, and it does bring some problems into our lives. The word wound means, *"damage, a grievance, a harm, an injury."* In essence, it is saying, "I've been wronged," "I've been hurt," "I've been abused." There are women who have been psychologically abused as well as physically abused. These women have deep down, unattended wounds that keep festering up, boiling up and causing problems. These wounds get their thoughts to go in the wrong direction. Thus, we think the wrong things, we feel the wrong things and we want to do those wrong things. There is hatred and unforgiveness, and it all goes back to those things, a wound in your life. Those wounds will grab your heart and force you to think on the wrong things. That's what happened a few moments before Christ was arrested, falsely accused and beaten. Christ was trying to prepare His chosen men. What happened? They got offended. The word "offend" is an interesting word in the Bible. The word *offend means, "to draw to evil; to cause to sin."* The best definition of the word *offend* that I've found is *"to push toward a transgression; to make to stumble."* This is what happens in our Christian lives. We have wounds and problems that we have not dealt with properly and appropriately. We are walking along, and, all of a sudden, we get wounded; we get hurt. Some of these wounds are not something we voted for but something that just came to us. It is our so-called "lot" in life. When they were passing out diabetes, I didn't say, "Gimme some of that! I want that!" Sometimes things just happen. Sometimes that divorce really did just happen, and when it was all over, your head was spinning because you just didn't see it coming.

Oh, by the way, I don't believe that if you get close to Jesus all those things are just going to disappear.

So, I can't do anything about the hurt, but what happens is that hurt grabs my attention. It causes me to stumble, trip and fall. So, I'm walking through life, and I get a hurt. Well, that hurt grabs my thoughts and meditations, but I am still walking through life. However, I am walking sideways, and I fall, I trip and I stumble. It all starts with a hurt, and what does that hurt do? It leads to an offense, and do you know what that offense does? It gives our mind permission to think things we should not think and do things we should not do. "Well, my wife isn't meeting my needs, so I'm just going to go to the gentlemen's club. One time won't hurt. Nobody will know. No one will see." It all started right there with a hurt. The hurt then led to an offense, and the offense gives permission in your mind to think things that you would not have otherwise thought. A fleshly appetite will always accompany permission in your mind. The Spirit, indeed, is willing, but the flesh is weak. Paul said in Romans 7:19-21, *"For the good that I would I do not: but the evil which I would not, that I do. Now if I do that I would not, it is no more I that do it, but sin that dwelleth in me. I find then a law, that, when I would do good, evil is present with me."* In other words, there is always an opportunity to do wrong. Paul went on to say in verse 24, *"O wretched man that I am, who shall deliver me from the body of this death?"* In the timeframe that Paul wrote this, if a man was murdered, especially a wealthy man, they would find the murderer, strip a freshly dead corpse naked, strip you naked, lay you face to face, chest to chest, thigh to thigh and wrap and tie you to that corpse. They would give you just enough food and water to drink until that old, bloating body strapped to you would rot, corrupt and finally ooze fluids and maggots. The oozing fluid from the dead body would slowly kill you. This was one of the cruelest deaths that you could have experienced in those times. Don't you think Paul would have seen this happening since he spent a lot of time in the various prisons around Rome? Now, do you understand what Paul was saying when he wrote that passage? He was saying that he is chained to a dead man; a dead man that is always dragging him down. Paul went on to say in verse 25, *"I thank God through Jesus Christ our Lord. So then with the mind I myself serve the law of God; but with the flesh the law of sin."* Always remember that it all starts with a wound and that wound leads to an offense. Once that offense gives permission to the mind, that permission in the mind is then accompanied with a fleshly appetite. This always sets the wheels in motion to do evil.

One of the most heart-breaking things that I have to deal with is baby Christians wanting to live for God, but, everywhere they turn, there's an opportunity to go back and do evil. Mark 14:38 says, *"Watch ye and pray, lest ye enter into temptation. The spirit truly is ready, but the flesh is weak."* The problem is, though, when we do go back and do wrong, we try and justify it. We tell ourselves, "It's okay this one time. Just one more! I got away with it last time. Just one more puff or one more drink won't hurt." By the time we get to this point in our thinking, we've already done it; we are already there. So, we do what's wrong, and our conscience begins to rebuke us. Not only does our conscience rebuke us, but, if we are a child of God, the Holy Spirit begins to convict us as well. If we can do wrong and sin and the Holy Spirit of God does not convict us, then we need to make sure we are saved. My Bible tells me that God chastens those He loves. He chastens those who belong to Him and those who call Him Father. If He does not tell you when you are doing wrong, then the Bible states you are of your father the devil. John 8:44 says, *"Ye are of your father the devil, and the lusts of your father ye will do."*

Finally, after we do wrong, we try to save face. We try to cover it up. We don't want to be embarrassed so we lie, connive, scheme and do whatever we can to get out of our dilemma. And, we do all this only to start all over again. "Well, I'm going to join the army." Well, my friend, the hurt is only going to go with you. "I'm going to move to ..." Again, the hurt will only move with you. "I'm going to get another spouse," Sorry, the hurt is still there no matter how many wives or husbands you get. All these things you think will make a difference will not make any difference because the wound, the hurt, goes with you. You MUST deal with it! Wherever you go, whatever you do, that wound is going to go with you. You have to deal with that wound. You can't break it after the offense. Once you start tripping your way through life, it's hard to break it after the offense. Then, the fleshly appetite kicks in, and it is hard to stop the flesh. You can't stop it after the opportunity because your two-thirds of the way there. You have to create some distance between the wound and the offense. The only thing that will create distance between a wound and an offense is a person named Jesus Christ. My friends, Isaiah 53:5 says, *"But he was wounded for our transgressions, he was bruised for our iniquities: the chastisement of our peace was upon him; and with his stripes we are healed."* WOW! There are not 12 steps or 10 steps. There is only ONE step! That ONE STEP is Jesus Christ. If you are not sure that if you died today you would go to heaven, you need to quit playing games with yourself. You need to get that issue settled today.

When I was pastoring, my son came to me, and he made a public profession. Shortly after, I had the privilege of baptizing him. Four or five years later in our ministry, we had a special speaker for chapel at our school, and he was speaking on revival, the rapture and various other things. My son, Josh, came home from school while I was in my study. He knocked on my door and asked if he could talk to me for a minute. I said, "Sure man, come on in!" He asked me what I remembered about him getting saved. I told him, "Son, it doesn't matter what I remember about you getting saved." I went on to tell him that what mattered was what he remembered

about getting saved." About 35 or 40 minutes later my son trusted Christ as his personal Savior. My personal conviction is this: When a person meets the Lord and Master, they remember where they met Him. He makes a lasting impression. You ought to be able to say, "I know the spot." It is not something that evolves or something that just happens. It is something that is very real and very personal. It is holy ground. Yes, I remember the day I gave my life to Jesus Christ. In 1976 I was at my next-door neighbor's house for a five-day club. All the other kids went up for their Kool-aid and toy for the day, but I stayed behind with Mike Reynolds who was the leader of our club. While I was there with Mr. Reynolds, I bowed my head and heart and trusted Christ as my personal Savior.

In summarizing my earlier comments, after a person gets saved, they need to make distance between the wound and the offense. This is called the "hidden life." It is called the crucified Christian life. This is when you say, "Ssshhh, settle down flesh; quiet down." The thing you must realize is that when you go through difficulties, when you go through tough days, when you get those wounds and those hurts, and, they are going to come, you must stay close to the Shepherd. You stay close to Christ. Stay close to the leaders that follow Christ. Stay close to your pastor, your spouse, your parents and anyone else in authority over you, because God is going to use them to help you with that next step, and that next step and that next step. You won't be offended if you stay close to the Shepherd! I am going to turn the page a little and tell you about when I first got married. Now, you need to understand that I was 11 years old before we had indoor plumbing. YES! I had an outhouse when I was little. When I got married, I lived in Gary, Indiana; the armpit of America and murder capital of the world. My new wife and I got ourselves a little apartment, and we were preparing to eat the first meal that she had cooked in our new apartment. I went upstairs and washed my hands. A few minutes before the meal started, my wife called me back upstairs. I went up there into the bathroom and I said, "Yea, what's up?" She said, "These towels right here are not to use. They are for show." I had never heard of anything like that. What do you mean "for show?" Remember what I mentioned earlier? I was used to growing up with only an outhouse, and we used to have a Sears-Roebuck Catalog in that outhouse! I was offended. The next morning I woke up, went to the bathroom and opened the medicine cabinet. Low and behold, "someone" (maybe my wife?) in my house had squeezed the toothpaste right in the middle. You don't squeeze the toothpaste in the middle! Everybody knows you squeeze the toothpaste from the end up.

I know those are silly illustrations, but there are husbands and wives in our churches today that are falling into temptation because they have feelings against each other. They harbor bitterness and unforgiveness, and the flesh is just eating them up. We all need to stay close to the Shepherd. There are teenagers who have parents who don't always make the right decisions. Sometimes they say yes when they should say no, and they say no when they should be saying yes! I tell my teenager, who is 14 years old, 6 foot tall and wears a size 12.5 shoe, "Son, I've never had anybody like you. You have to be patient with me, man." We were watching a ball game just the other day, and a player got ejected. Their team was up 21 points, and they lost the game in the fourth quarter, after the player got ejected because he got wounded and then he got offended. I used that as an illustration in my son's life as not to let this happen to him. I told him to stay close to mom and dad, because we can help him through this thing called life. We may not always make the right choices and decisions. There are teenagers in our churches who, when their parents ask them to do something, their attitude is "whatever!" Don't let it be "whatever" but let it be a "passion" because that's my mom and dad, my God-given authority.

There are thousands of illustrations I can give, but I need to get this out: Do you want to know why Reformers Unanimous is such a wonderful ministry? It gets people back to the Shepherd. They find a role model to look up to in their director and in their leader. Those who love the Lord will help you serve the Lord, and those who don't love the Lord won't help you serve the Lord.

In this life we are going to be offended, have hurts, experience difficulties and the like. But, to paraphrase our Lord and Savior, He is trying to tell us, "Sit here." I know it hurts. I know you want to get up and run. I know what you want to do but just sit down and be quiet for a little while." The distance Christ is trying to get us to see is for one reason and that reason is for the wicked flesh to die, to go to the cross daily and say, "It is not always about me; it's about Him." Sssshhhh, hush. Don't spout off at the mouth. Don't get in the car and spin the wheels. Don't get into debt. Don't do it. Hush and sit down. Turn your eyes upon Jesus and look into His wonderful face, and the things of earth will grow strangely dim. SIT, WATCH and PRAY.

Remember the story of Joseph? His brothers despised him and set out to hurt him. You talk about wounds! Joseph had a pile of them. However, when his brothers came begging for food years later, they recognized their brother and were scared for their lives. Paraphrasing, Joseph said, "Don't worry fellas. What you meant for evil, God meant for good." This is an example of true forgiveness. The truth is we need a good dose of it in our churches today. Dr. David Gibbs taught me that forgiveness is a legal term. It has nothing to do with our feelings or emotions. It's a legal term. Forgiveness says, "I'm going to release you. I'm not going to bring it up to you. I'm not going to bring it up to others. I'm not even going to allow myself to meditate on it. I am releasing you." A lot of individuals say, "Well I can forgive but I can't forget." You missed the Biblical point altogether. The Bible says in Luke 23:34, *"Father, forgive them; for they know not what they do."* The Bible also says in Ephesians 4:32, *"And be ye kind one to another, tenderhearted, forgiving one another, even as God for Christ's sake hath forgiven you."* Some are harboring bitterness and unforgiveness in their hearts because they don't believe that God's forgiveness is very big. The truth is some of us need to cancel our pity party today. "Nobody likes me; everyone hates me." Okay, we don't like you! We really don't so just get over it! You need to get over it, and regardless of what happens, you need to learn to say, "Whatever my lot, thou hast taught me to say, it is well with my soul." Forgiveness is a BIG KEY to healing the hurts in your life. Forgive those who offend you, and forgive those who hurt you. Only when you forgive and forget can God start working in your life with a power that is so dynamic. FORGIVE AND START WALKING IN GOD'S POWER! It's awesome!

Appendix C

Getting Down to the Heart of the Matter

*I*N GENESIS 22, GOD ASKED ABRAHAM TO take his son, Isaac, to a mountain in Moriah and offer him up for a sacrifice. At the time Isaac was not a small child. He was around 25 years old. Isaac asked his father, *"Where is the lamb for a burnt offering?"* And Abraham answered, *"My son, God will provide himself a lamb for a burnt offering."* When God saw that Abraham was willing to sacrifice his "only" son for Him, He stopped him and provided a ram instead.

In the Bible we find many different types of relationships that man can have with God. The first type of relationship we find is with God the Creator. There are some people out there that do not have that relationship, such as atheists and those who believe we evolved. When I was in college, I used to go soul winning at Purdue University. My soul winning partner, who was a professor at my bible college, met a man there who was on the debate team. He wanted to have a debate with the professor on Creationism vs. Darwinism. When they got together to have the debate, the preacher went first. He asked the question, "Where does man come from?" The man from the university answered, "He came from the primate family." Then, the preacher asked, "Where does the primate family came from?" The man from the university replied, "The primate family came from lower life forms." When the preacher asked, "Where did the lower life forms came from?" The man from the university replied, "They came from the cooling of hydrogen and oxygen." When the preacher asked, "What caused the cooling?" The university man said, "The big bang." He insisted that the "big bang" was caused by cosmic dust. Finally, the preacher asked, "Where did the cosmic dust come from?" The professor had no explanation. He said that it just had always been there. That part of the debate was over, and it was the preacher's turn to answer the questions. When asked where man came from, he turned to Genesis, chapter one, and showed where God had created man. "The difference is," he said, "You believe in a big bowl of dust, and I believe in a big, wonderful God."

However, if we only acknowledge God as our Creator, there is something wrong. He is the creator, but He is also the rewarder of those who diligently seek Him. **The first type of relationship with God is a relationship with God the Creator and Rewarder.** Hebrews 11:6 says, "But without faith it is impossible to please him: for he that cometh to God must believe that he is, and that he is a rewarder of them that diligently seek him." If God is only a creator to you, you will not go to heaven. You are a sinner, and the wages of sin is death. Going to church and Sunday school is not enough to save you from hell. Even getting baptized and becoming a church member is not enough. Only the blood of Jesus is enough to save your soul.

The second type of relationship with God is a relationship with God the Redeemer. When we accept Jesus Christ as our Savior, He makes a lasting impression on our lives. I can take you to the exact spot where I got saved. You should be able to remember where you got saved and revisit that place often in your mind.

A third type of relationship you can have with God is with Him as your God. When you recognize that God is your god and that you are one of his people, there is a change that takes place in you. You will want to become separated from the world. This separation happens because you are no longer a part of the world's family; you are part of God's family. The world is a temporary place for you, and your eternal home is in heaven.

Fourthly, there is also a relationship with God as the Father. The Bible says that we call him Abba Father. We bear the name of Christ. This is why we are called "Christians." We even have a relationship with God as Lord. This means He is our Master; He is our Boss. Because He is Lord, we have a duty to obey every one of His commands, if for no other reason than because He said so.

The last and closest of all our relationships with God is the relationship with God our friend; the kind of friend Abraham had. We can achieve this relationship with God by always trying to reach the next level with Him. Once we are committed to the cause of Christ, it is often too late to turn back. We should not be ashamed of the Gospel of Christ and what God is doing in our lives.

The pursuit of God is the greatest pursuit anyone could ever have. I get dumbfounded sometimes when I see what people do to get another hit, sniff, push, drink or snort of a drug. The pursuit people have of worldly possessions is far too strong. We should pursue that way after God. He is the One we should long for and chase after. However, there is a danger in reaching new levels in Christ. I have been preaching the Word of God for 28 years. I've seen a lot of people who are on fire for God, and then they turn around and go the other way. I ran from God for a year and a half when I was sixteen years old. I was as backslidden as a person can get.

The pursuit of God always begins with the heart. The Lord wants us to love Him with all our heart. God doesn't look at the outside; he doesn't see if we are dressed up on Sunday or not. He looks at the inside. I was eating dinner on Wednesday night with my son, who is a 16-year-old senior in high school. I asked for the combination to his locker. He asked what I needed it for, and I told him I wanted to go check some things out. He willingly gave me the combination and assured me that I would not find anything out of the ordinary. I snoop in everything my kids do. That's because I'm the parent, and he's the child. Some of you parents better wake up because some of your children have you fooled. You need to investigate their computers. Look at the temporary Internet files. Find out what they are saying and doing on Facebook. Don't be worried about the kids getting mad. I'd rather have them be mad than have them be without the truth of God. We give our children plenty of mercy, and they feel it coming from us. We give them good meals and a place to live. There must be truth that accompanies our mercy. God wants the keys to our heart because it is desperately wicked. The heart is a volatile place. It is where murders are pondered and lust is conceived. We are told this in Matthew 15:19: *"For out of the heart proceed evil thoughts, murders, adulteries, fornications, thefts, false witness, blasphemies:"* It bubbles and it smolders. The same thing is reiterated in Mark 7:2, which says, *"For from within, out of the heart of men, proceed evil thoughts, adulteries, fornications, murders."*

God wants the key to your heart. He will open it and see everything that is going on inside. You can not pull the wool over God's eyes. Revival is not going to come to our nations or our churches until we turn our keys over to God and let him get down to business. Your sin will find you out eventually.

God is found when our hearts are fully exposed to us and to Him. We can go to the next level with Him when we can look at the same thing He is looking at, and we can call it the same thing He calls it. When God looks at our hearts, He looks at our motives. When we do good things, God is displeased if it is being done for the wrong reasons. After our hearts are fully exposed, God desires to take us to the next level. God fully expects us to show Him a love that exceeds any other love which is found in our hearts. Our love for anyone or anything else should pale in comparison to our love for God. The Bible says to whom much is forgiven, love much. If we would meditate more on how much God has forgiven us, we would begin to clean up our hearts. God knows the wickedness that is in our hearts. Genesis 6:5 says, "And God saw that the wickedness of man was great in the earth, and that every imagination of the thoughts of his heart was only evil continually." Genesis 8:21 says, "...for the imagination of man's heart is evil from his youth..." God wants to wipe us clean. Psalm 51:10 says, "Create in me a clean heart, O God; and renew a right spirit within me." Jeremiah 17:9 says, "The heart is deceitful above all things, and desperately wicked: who can know it?"

The Bible says in Matthew 6:21, "For where your treasure is, there will your heart be also." If our hearts are good, we will do what is good. Matthew 12:35 says, "A good man out of the good treasure of the heart bringeth forth good things: and an evil man out of the evil treasure bringeth forth evil things." Show me what you did with your checkbook this week, and I'll show you how much you love God. God is doing some great things in churches. However, in many churches, only about ten percent of the people tithe. You might say that you can't afford to tithe. How can you afford not to tithe? It may not bother your preacher that you don't tithe. But, when God turns the key to your heart and shows you your failed tithing record, it's time to go to the next level. Anything you give that is less than ten percent of what you made this week is just a tip. Anything less will show you what your heart is really investing in. We live in a world that is dying and going to hell, and a lack of finances is one of the things that hold churches back from doing the work of God.

God asks you to fully exceed the love and devotion that He sees in your heart toward those things to be redirected to Him. The Bible says in Matthew 15:8, *"This people draweth nigh unto me with their mouth, and honoureth me with their lips; but their heart is far from me."* In Matthew 15:18, He says, *"But those things which proceed out of the mouth come forth from the heart; and they defile the man."* There are some of us that fuss and complain far too often. If you want to go to the next level with God, you must give him the key. Matthew 13:15 says, *"For this people's heart is waxed gross, and their ears are dull of hearing, and their eyes they have closed; lest at any time they should see with their eyes, and hear with their ears, and should understand with their heart, and should be converted, and I should heal them."* There are some that have heard the Gospel again and again and have continually resisted getting saved. You've walked on your way, and God is telling you that you have come too far this time. He wants the key. I gave my key to God for the first time in 1976. He took one look and told me I needed a Savior that could reach down in the miry clay and set me free. And, my friend, that is what you need too.

Now, you might ask, "How did I get all that out of Abraham?" At least 25 years earlier God told Abraham that he was going to be the father of a great nation. The Bible says that Abraham got down on his knees and laughed in his heart. Because Abraham was one hundred years old and his wife was ninety, He thought that was the funniest thing he had ever heard. The reason God asked Abraham to give his only son was because God wanted to take him to the next level. God looked at his heart, and He saw how much Isaac meant to him. That's why He didn't ask for Ishmael. Ishmael was in illegitimate child. Some of you need to reach in to your Spiritual pockets and hand over your key to God. You don't have to be worried; God is full of mercy. His love never fails, and His mercy endures forever. If you cover your heart and hide it from God, He will rip the cover right off. He will expose you for what you really are. If He wasn't embarrassed to expose our sin at the cross on Calvary 2,000 years ago, He certainly isn't embarrassed to do it now.

The thing I like the most about Reformers Unanimous is that we don't just deal with one sin. The problem with AA is that they only deal with one sin. You are never going to find help if you try to fix just one small area of your life. You're never going to recover in a program that never wants to talk about being recovered. They want you to believe that you are always recovering. You are not going to find recovery by sitting around a table and talking about your problems yet doing nothing about them. Whoever Christ makes free is freed indeed. The reason you keep going back to the pig pen is that you have not claimed the freedom that is found in Jesus Christ. If all God is to you is a Creator, He is telling you to give Him your key. He wants to help you.

Proverbs 6:18 – *"An heart that deviseth wicked imaginations, feet that be swift in running to mischief."*

Proverbs 21:4 – *"An high look, and a proud heart, and the plowing of the wicked, is sin."*

Matthew 12:34 – *"O generation of vipers, how can ye, being evil, speak good things? for out of the abundance of the heart the mouth speaketh."*

Matthew 5:28 – *"But I say unto you, That whosoever looketh on a woman to lust after her hath committed adultery with her already in his heart."*

Matthew 15:8 – *"This people draweth nigh unto me with their mouth, and honoureth me with their lips; but their heart is far from me."*

Matthew 15:18 – *"But those things which proceed out of the mouth come forth from the heart; and they defile the man."*

Matthew 22:37 – *"Jesus said unto him, Thou shalt love the Lord thy God with all thy heart, and with all thy soul, and with all thy mind."*

Matthew 5:8 – *"Blessed are the pure in heart: for they shall see God."*

Hebrews 10:22 – *"Let us draw near with a true heart in full assurance of faith, having our hearts sprinkled from an evil conscience, and our bodies washed with pure water."*

ABOUT THE AUTHOR

Dr. George T. Crabb, D.O.,
Addiction Medicine Specialist

Dr. George T. Crabb is a Board Certified Internal Medicine physician and a Fellow of the American College of Osteopathic Internist. He practices Internal Medicine and Addiction Medicine in Naples, Florida. He is a member of the American Society of Addiction Medicine, the American Osteopathic Academy of Addiction Medicine and the Florida Osteopathic Medical Association.

Dr. Crabb serves as the Medical Advisor to Reformers Unanimous Recovery Ministries. He has an active pulpit ministry and frequently speaks abroad representing Reformers Unanimous. Dr. Crabb conducts seminars and has authored several books and numerous booklets on a wide range of medical and spiritual topics. Many of which are available on **drgeorgecrabb.com** or **reformersrecovery.com/store**

Dr. Crabb is an ordained Baptist minister. He served with his father (Pastor George Crabb, Antioch Baptist) as an assistant for 20 years. He is the author of the book, "Just Say Know, God's Answer to Addiction" published by Reformers Unanimous.

MORE BOOKS FROM BY THE AUTHOR

Just Say Know

God's Answer to Addiction
by Dr. George T. Crabb, D.O.
CE-125
Foreword by Steven B. Curington

Whether you battle with drugs, nicotine, alcohol, pornography, gambling, or any other habitual sin, God's answer is to just say know. You may learn all the facts about addiction that society could ever teach, but this fact remains true: it's not what you know, it's Who you know. Jesus said, "and ye shall know the truth, and the truth shall make you free."

Jesus Christ can make you free. He can break through the doubts, despair, and depression of your life. This book will remind us who we are as children of God. As children of God, we have been offered many things in Christ Jesus. Among them are life, liberty, and eternal happiness. If these wonderful gifts seem out of reach, it could be the biggest mistake of our lives to underestimate their availability to us.

In an effort to explain our easy access to the abundant Christian life, I want to help you understand the battle that is going on for your mind. This one battle is the battle of all battles. It is the battle that our victory is most predicated upon. With this battle won, victory is eminent. To be alive and free in Christ is the birthright of every Christian. May we learn to reject the deceiver's offer to exchange our birthright for a temporary filling of a particular pleasure.

Addiction: The Facts

Dr. George T. Crabb D.O.
& Steven B. Curington
# RB-117 $11.⁹⁵

A new series of fifteen topical books on addiction. Bro. Curington and his trusted medical advisor, Dr. George Crabb D.O., break apart the effects that addiction plays on the body, the soul, and the spirit. By introducing the full gospel of justification, sanctification, and glorification to the recovering addict, they learn the effects that Jesus Christ can produce within our spirit, soul, and body.

List of All Topical Books:

Cocaine	TRB-001	Gambling	TRB-010
Alcohol	TRB-002	Prescription Meds	TRB-011
Meth	TRB-003	Heroin	TRB-012
Weed	TRB-004	Acid	TRB-013
Cutting	TRB-005	Huffing	TRB-014
Pornography	TRB-006	Steroids	TRB-015
Uppers	TRB-007		
Tobacco	TRB-008	**All topical books are** $4.⁰⁰ **each**	
Eating Disorders	TRB-009	**or one complete set for $45.⁰⁰**	

Retail Set: Includes 3 copies of each Topical Book + Display
TRB-000.................................... $149.⁰⁰

Reach your addicted friends or loved-ones in a safe and non-invasive way!

$79.00
KIT-001

Many of you have undoubtedly had a burden to reach friends and loved-ones who are struggling with addiction. Unfortunately, reaching out to an addict is not an easy thing to do. Often, personal contact with an addict is unwelcomed, and even worse, can be dangerous to initiate. Too often, we are left feeling helpless as we watch a loved-one spiral down a destructive cycle of addiction. We at RU have sought to develop a perceptive tool to help overcome this problem. Introducing the Personal Recovery Kit—an intuitive method designed to reach out to hurting people in a gentle, non-threatening way. This kit is specifically formulated to empower the addict by providing them with tools that are proven to help overcome addiction.

This proven method is a great way to introduce your loved-one to the life-saving ministry of Reformers Unanimous in a simple, non-invasive manner. Ask God if He would have you intervene in your loved one's life, and allow Reformers Unanimous to present the saving power of Jesus Christ in an easy and convenient way. Do not delay, my friends…lives rest in the balance!!!

The Personal Recovery Kit Includes:

▶ Topical Addiction Recovery Book (15 topics from which to choose: from alcohol, cocaine, meth, marijuana, cutting, pornography, stimulants, tobacco, eating disorders, gambling, prescription meds, heroin, acid, huffing, and steroids)

▶ Spiritual Recovery Journal w/ instructional CD

▶ Spiritual Recovery Textbook

▶ 10 Spiritual Recovery Principles DVD

▶ Spiritual Recovery Program Workbook

▶ Bitterness and Forgiveness Recovery Series on MP3 CD

▶ Spiritual Recovery Mega-Pack on MP3 CD (Includes topical teaching on: wrong thinking, depression, forgiveness, Rx addiction, sexual addiction, opiates, and dozens of other topics.)

call 815-986-0460
or visit www.personalrecoverykit.com

Reformers Unanimous
RECOVERY MINISTRIES